By buying this book you are directly supporting
the mission of Green Card Voices.

"*Green Card Youth Voices* is a book I wish I had growing up as a first-generation Filipina-American in the Midwest. Students who are featured share their powerful immigration stories with clarity and humility; allowing any reader to understand their journey to the United States as well as the value they add to our communities. This book is for all Americans—no matter the birthplace. Green Card Voices brings visibility to the promise of America—a place where those yearning for freedom can find a new home and create a better tomorrow for their families and for our communities." **—Paula Phillips, Milwaukee Board of Schools Director District 7**

"Not only is the experience of telling one's personal narrative empowering to immigrant youth, but hearing them speak in their own words helps the reader put themselves in the storyteller's shoes, even if their own lived experience is not similar in any way to what these youth are dealing with—their words beautifully illustrate the contradictions between feelings of cultural and social isolation but even in the face of the challenges, the educational motivation to stay and pursue their educational and professional dreams." **—Elizabeth Tryon, Assistant Director, Community-Engaged Scholarship at the Morgridge Center, University of Wisconsin-Madison**

"The stories shared in *Green Card Youth Voices: Immigration Stories from Madison and Milwaukee High Schools* are powerful, inspiring and shining examples of why giving our youth a platform to share their voices is critical. I hope by seeing the collection of essays in this book, more young people are compelled to speak up and advocate for themselves, their families and the issues important to them." **— Kathy Thornton-Bias, President & CEO, Boys & Girls Clubs of Greater Milwaukee**

"*Green Card Youth Voices: Immigration Stories from Madison and Milwaukee High Schools* is the one book that truly helps me know my neighbors. I'm inspired by the journeys of the young people in this book. I'll read the stories again and again. It's rare to find such an honest account of the young life of an immigrant. This book should be provided for all educators to better understand the life of students coming from other countries." **—Kelly Schaer, Program Director, College Possible–Milwaukee**

"*Green Card Youth Voices* is the only resource I can think of that stitches together the voices, stories, hopes, and possibilities of youth from so many migration and immigration experiences in such concrete and humanizing ways. As youth share their stories and the visions they have for their futures and the futures of their families and communities, this book becomes a living world of what it means to be a part of the dynamic communities of southern Wisconsin. I hope all teachers and future teachers listen carefully to what is being shared in these pages—and that we all find ways to bring them into our classrooms, so that we as educators can better come to know the young people we have the privilege of teaching and learning alongside every day." **—Jenna Cushing-Leubner, Ph.D., Assistant Professor of Languages Education, Director of Certificate in Heritage Language Education, University of Wisconsin–Whitewater**

"The stories included in *Green Card Youth Voices: Immigration Stories from Madison and Milwaukee High Schools* strengthen our knowledge of the inclusivity and diversity often so invisible in Wisconsin. In telling their stories, these young writers empower themselves and their families by sharing their journeys to Wisconsin and where those journeys will lead them. These are the kinds of stories that allow readers to vision new worlds but, at the same time, allow us to vision our worlds anew by recognizing who contributes to our communities. Green Card Voices is a resource to teach in classrooms to address and develop respect for the rich diversity evident throughout Wisconsin, in young writers academies as models of personal narrative that empower youth to tell their stories, or to just plain curl up in a chair and read and enjoy the journeys of the courageous people who come to America." **—Donna L. Pasternak, Professor of English Education, University of Wisconsin-Madison**

"The power of every individual lies in their story and this rings especially true in Green Card Voices. I was moved and inspired by the stories of young immigrants who call Wisconsin home. Their narratives are a powerful example of what makes America a beacon of hope and opportunity for so many. Given the growing anti-immigrant climate, their stories serve as an important reminder of how much immigrants shape and strengthen America's identity. Their storytelling should deepen our empathy and understanding of the immigrant experience. I am proud of Milwaukee's rich history of creating diverse communities where immigrants prosper. Milwaukeeans and Madisonites know the unique individuals who enrich our communities, and Green Card allows others to see it."　　　　　　　　　　　**—Gwen S. Moore, Member of Congress**

"The power of words can tear down or build up humanity. In the current anti-immigrant climate, we are hearing narrative after narrative of hate, xenophobia, and disdain for immigrants, which is dehumanizing people who are no different than the immigrants in the first or second wave of immigration to the US in the 1800s. Green Card Voices stories continue to tell the stories of the same 'America' with the same dreams, yearning to be free. The voices in this book belong to high school students who live in Madison and Milwaukee. They tell the counter-narrative to hate and shed light on humanity telling of their own acts of courage and unwavering hope but with humility and dignity."　　　**—Ruslana Westerlund, EdD Ukrainian-American Author, Speaker &**
Education Researcher at WIDA, University of Wisconsin-Madison

"The courageous young people sharing their personal journeys in *Green Card Youth Voices* are our classmates, our neighbors and our family members. They are our communities' past, present and future. For Wisconsin to truly thrive, we must listen with care and attention to the narratives of those whose cultural context and experiences differ from our own. In an incredible act of generosity, these young storytellers have opened the door to their worlds, so that we can better understand the wider world and the humanity we all share."
—Ellen M. Gilligan, President & CEO, Greater Milwaukee Foundation

"Though independent testimonials, I see clear parallels in these stories to that of my own. Drawing these connections are how we begin to dismantle the structures and silos in our community and it gives me great pride in knowing that these voices of hope and resilience are our future generation. I applaud *Green Card Youth Voices* for maintaining the integrity of our immigrant youth in a piece that reminds us of the importance of inclusivity in an increasingly diverse population. At this moment in history, it is imperative that these stories of unforgettable strength, courage and humility continue to be shared."　　　　　**—Faatima Khan, Director of Corporate &**
Community Engagement, United Way of Dane County

"I am very impressed and highly recommend this book of Green Card Voices of stories on the immigration experiences of students from Madison and Milwaukee. It is fascinating that the past few years have seen a renewed focus on the stories of young immigrants as they come to America. Books on similar narratives are being published in other communities. There are significant similarities between these youthful voices. These stories cause an immersion into their lives of struggles for survival and acceptance; with identity, race, culture and language; and their dreams and hopes for more education and a better tomorrow. There are many things we would not know were it not for these publications, and they need to continue. There is a lot we can do to change our education systems to embrace this diversity in an America that must learn how to embrace it, respect it, and allow it to make us more understanding and better human beings. Those of us who want our schools and universities to be better places of learning and empathy must draw on these narrations to best inform why we need a world without false borders, especially when the views on migrations we hold today and why the huge migrations we experience are often the result of what we do as a country elsewhere."
—Tony Báez, Vice-President, Milwaukee Public Schools Board of Directors

"I first started working with migrant students in 1986 at West High School in Madison, Wisconsin, as a teacher assistant—this was a group of fifteen amazing and courageous minors who were taken away with assistance from United Migrants Opportunity Services (UMOS) from a farm in Oregon, Wisconsin for mistreating them. I am still in communication with most them and have been a mentor for their new American families throughout the years. These immigrants have been change agents and their personal stories must be read and being heard, they are the true new American and are representatives of what this country is made of—immigrants."

—**Alejandro Nuñez, Education Director, English Language Learning, Wisconsin Technical College System**

"The power of diverse and inclusive storytelling resonates throughout these pages. Growing up in this country as a daughter of immigrants has meant that I have been over exposed to a plethora of euro-centric stories that erase, ignore and sometimes deny the truths of communities of color around the world; including those of my own people. By being vulnerable enough to share their stories, these young people call us all to action. They call on us to listen. They call on us to a deeper awareness and curiosity about the people that we see in our communities every day. They call on us to reflect on the framing and the lens stories we unconsciously ingest and those that we must continue to seek out and highlight. Ultimately, they call us to the powerful act of self-reflection. Reflecting on your story, your identity and your connection to the larger world around you is a valuable first step for growth, meaningful connection, healing and wholeheartedness. This compilation gives credence to the idea that the stories of the young people in our community matter and that their power will move us all forward."

—**Meralis Hood, Executive Director, City Year Milwaukee**

"*Green Card Youth Voices* should be a mandatory reading for all students starting high school. This is a time when we are figuring out who we are and where we belong in this new stage of our lives. Now take it a step further. It isn't just a new school. Now it's a new world. It's a new language, a new culture, a new home. It is so wonderful to hear how it works from the perception of high school students as they continue to work through all of these additional barriers to becoming an adult. And the young people in this book do it in such an interesting and engaging way. The narrative really helps you to wonder about what happens next? And what does the future bring? The book also helps us to think about the parents, siblings, other family and folks left back home. So many come to the US to be safe. It is lovely to hear about how this is happening to many youth in our communities."

—**Dawn Berney, Executive Director of Jewish Social Services of Madison, Refugee Resettlement Agency in Madison, WI**

"Today, more than ever, we need to hear ALL voices. Green Card Voices gives voice to those most immediately and personally impacted by the immigration crisis...students themselves. It is a compelling book and one I highly recommend reading."

—**Susan Ela, Retired COO Aurora Health Care**

"*Green Card Youth Voices* is an excellent resource for educators interested in bringing global perspectives into the classroom. The accounts of young people from so many countries powerfully demonstrate the interconnection between communities in Wisconsin and the rest of the world. Readers are left with an appreciation of both the diversity of the human experience and our shared humanity."

—**Nicole Palasz, Program Coordinator, Institute of World Affairs, University of Wisconsin-Milwaukee**

"First, we find permission to claim value in our own narrative. From there, we gift ourselves and the worlds around us by honoring every page of our life story. This endeavor will have an enormous impact on how we trade histories and remind us to reach for the richness on the other side of our own knowing."

—**Dasha Kelly Hamilton, Poet, Author & Executive Director, Still Waters Collective**

Green Card Youth Voices

Immigration Stories from Madison and Milwaukee High Schools

Stephanie Salgado, Vy Luong, Christine Encarnacion, Nana-Kwesi Konadu, Ruqayah Alkhrsa, Yanci Almonte Vargas, Selma Fustok, Harield Acuna, Dickshya Gurung, Alirio Romero, Edman Ahmed, Tenzin Rangdol, Ana Fernandez Roque, Kou Yang, Juweriya Hassen, Alain Quezadas, Bibi Sadeeqa Sulaimankhel, Aziz Kamal, Moo Eh Paw, Shaheed Dhawheed, Najaris Hernandez-Martinez, Annuwar Hussein, Htoo Ktray Wah, Uk Lian Thawng, Nur Fatema Nor Bashar, Chadier Figueroa Feliciano, Marjida Bi, Jonathan Cordero Torres, Ko Mu Ku, Mohammad Huzaifa

Authors

Tea Rozman Clark, Jessie Lee-Bauder
Editors

ISBN 13: 978-1-949523-12-6
eISBN 13: 978-1-949523-13-3
LCCN: 2018932723

Printed in the United States of America
First Printing: 2019
20   19 18   17   16   5   4   3   2   1

Edited by Tea Rozman Clark, Jessie Lee-Bauder

Cover design by Elena Dodevska
Interior design by Shiney Chi-Ia Her

Photography, videography by Media Active: Youth Produced Media

Green Card Voices
2611 1st Avenue South
Minneapolis, MN 55408
www.greencardvoices.org

Consortium Book Sales & Distribution
34 Thirteenth Avenue NE, Suite 101
Minneapolis, MN 55413-1007
www.cbsd.com

We dedicate this book to all of the people who arrived amid heightened national conversations about our values surrounding the topics of race, religion, and immigration. By sharing your stories, you demonstrate the importance of inclusivity and building the platform for a culture of understanding and empathy. Never doubt for a second that this is your home . . . you belong here.

Table of Contents

How to Use this Book

At the end of each student's essay, you will find a URL link to that student's digital narrative on Green Card Voices' website. You will also see a QR code link to that story. Below are instructions for using your mobile device to scan a QR code.

1. Open your phone camera and scan the QR code. If your phone camera cannot scan the code, using your mobile device—such as a smartphone or tablet—visit the App Store for your network, such as the Apple Store or the Android Store. Search the App Store for a "QR reader." You will find multiple free apps for you to download, and any one of them will work with this book.

2. Open your new QR reader app. Once the app has opened, hover the camera on your mobile device a few inches away from the QR code you want to scan. The app will capture the image of the QR code and take you to that student's profile page on the Green Card Voices website.

3. Once your web browser opens, you'll see the digital story. Press play and watch one of our inspirational stories.

STEP 1

Open up your phone camera OR download the app.

Available on the
App Store

Available on the Android
App Store

STEP 2

Scan the QR code.

STEP 3

Watch the digital story.

Foreword

Like the authors of this book, I also felt I had a story to tell as a young Chicano male living in the Midwest and growing up in the 1960's. I spent most of my time in predominantly white, Christian, and English speaking Wisconsin cities, like Racine, Milwaukee, Oshkosh and Madison. These experiences and recollections helped shape my awareness of the world, and helped me understand that despite the economic shortcomings of growing up with a family of 14 people, my life could not have been any richer.

When I first started writing, I didn't fully understand the impact that my writing would have on myself, or the world around me. My first challenge to overcome was learning to use my personal struggles to understand myself, and sharing those nuggets of wisdom with the world. I knew I wanted to share my insights with others through writing to both enlighten and entertain them. My early poems, "Elvis Presley was a Chicano", "History Lesson" and "My Mother is a Social Worker who works in a Hospital" were my attempts to understand how to best interpret what I was experiencing at that moment and try to connect with others through my stories and poems.

I didn't fully understand yet that while my writing journey was on a greater path to "know thyself," it could also have an impact on people who were not Chicano, those who didn't have shared experiences, or who never lived in Wisconsin.

Similarly, *Green Card Youth Voices: Immigration Stories from Madison and Milwaukee High Schools* provides a powerful forum for reading and experiencing personal narratives that remind us of how small the world really is, if we focus on our commonalities, not our differences.

You, the readers of the *Green Card Youth Voices* anthology, are given a chance to peek behind the curtain and hear authentic voices of young people struggling to find their way in an adopted country. Despite all the obstacles faced by immigrants, of language, culture, and at times poverty, they amazingly have found their path to success. These stories are what make America great.

This is the true power of Green Card Voices. This book will not only inform, impact and touch the reader, but also encourage these 30 young new authors into empowerment. This book provides a platform to inspire others to share their stories, helps us all find common ground in our shared experiences, and allows others to see these young writers become transformed right in front of our eyes.

By participating in this Green Card Youth Voices storytelling project, these students have the opportunity to see how much their writing can not only impact others, but also how this self reflection could be the catapult into the next phase of their young lives.

As the Editor of three anthologies titled *I Didn't Know There Were Latinos in Wisconsin*, Volumes 1-3 that spoke about the diverse Latino experience in Wisconsin over three decades, I believe that *Green Card Youth Voices: Immigration Stories from Madison and Milwaukee High Schools* continues the effort to share immigrant stories and personal narratives from families struggling to find their way in a new land.

Having lived and worked a considerable amount of time in both Milwaukee and Madison, two Wisconsin cities that are trying to balance gentrification, emerging communities and diverse populations, these personal stories share some of the hardships experienced when neighborhoods and cities are changing at a rapid pace.

These new voices cause us to pause and reflect on our past and present, but most importantly provide a path of hope for the future. Their optimism for tomorrow is contagious.

Oscar Mireles
Madison Poet Laureate, 2016 - present
Editor, *I Didn't Know There Were Latinos in Wisconsin*, Volumes 1-3
Executive Director, Omega School

Acknowledgments

To make this book possible, we have many individuals, organizations, and entities to thank.

The most important contributors to this project are the thirty authors who so courageously shared their stories. From hours of preparation in the classroom to bravely telling their stories on camera, from posing for portraits to working with coaches from College Possible Milwaukee, volunteers from the University of Wisconsin-Madison English Department, and teachers from their local high schools to polish their writing, these young authors have put forth tremendous effort in order to bring you these essays and video narratives. They are the heart and soul of this work. We are so grateful for and proud of them!

Pulaski High School and James Madison Memorial High School join with us and share our pride. We would like to thank the principals who lead each of the schools these young authors attend: Principal Matt Hendrickson (James Madison Memorial High School) and Principal Lolita Patrick (Pulaski High School). Our gratitude is multiplied to our school-site partners who helped us identify, recruit, orient, and prepare student authors for this work. Without your commitment to these authors and to this project, this book would not have been possible. Our honor roll of educators includes at the top of the list the following individuals: Christine Lemon and Robin Harris (Pulaski High School) and Leslie Mitchell (James Madison Memorial High School) as well as the College Possible Milwaukee coaches, Brittany Cannon and Tanja Skiljevic. We are also grateful for the help and support of Cynthia Price and Anne Knezevic (James Madison Memorial High School), who worked closely with EL students throughout the essay development process. Your enthusiasm for this project has not waivered—if anything, it has been strengthened throughout this experience. We are fortunate to have you guiding young people from all walks of life through public education.

In order to accomplish the amount of necessary work remotely from our office in neighboring Minnesota, the support of key local partners was crucial. We were fortunate to find an incredible partner in College Possible Milwaukee, especially Benjamin Precourt, a College Possible Milwaukee Program Coordinator who reached out in May 2018 to establish a partnership with

Green Card Voices. He told us about the stories to be shared in Milwaukee, telling us: "The students are amazing, and I strongly believe that their stories could be impactful for the greater Milwaukee community." He couldn't have been more right! Our team met with Ben and the College Possible Milwaukee Program Director, Kelly Schaer, in July 2018, and we began to realize how much both of our organizations and the communities we serve would benefit through our collaboration. A substantial and necessary portion of College Possible's work is the development of students' college essays—and while they were already able to support their students in this effort, they also struggled to find a process that ensured each student's life experiences shone through in writing. Green Card Voices' approach helped deliver essays that truly captured students' experiences and goals. Through our work with College Possible Milwaukee, we've not only developed a book but also empowered our authors to write strong essays that will help them attend college, receive scholarships, and succeed in their future endeavors.

On the other hand, our work in Madison with James Madison Memorial High School succeeded a different partnership. We'd worked in depth with the school just six months earlier in March of 2018, when they selected *Green Card Youth Voices: Immigration Stories from a Minneapolis High School* for their all-school read. As all 2,200 students at the school dove into our books and interacted with our videos and content, several of their teachers reached out and expressed a desire to have their students share their stories in a similar way. Thus, a partnership between Green Card Voices and James Madison Memorial High School was created.

Just as College Possible Milwaukee was our crucial partner in Milwaukee, the same was the case for the University of Wisconsin-Madison partners. Our deep gratitude goes to Caroline Carlson, a UW-Madison alumna who worked to support our project by securing volunteers and connections through the school's English Department; Karen Redfield, UW-Madison's English Department advisor; and Emily Hall, UW-Madison's Writing Fellows Director. Thank you to our incredible writing coaches/volunteers, UW-Madison English majors: Elizabeth Wahmhoff, Mark Salamone, Ariana King, Sam Wood, and Tye Trondson. They transcribed the essays, met with the authors on several occasions, and worked closely with them to help develop their essays.

To capture the authors' stories in their own words, Green Card Voices' (GCV) Executive Director, Tea Rozman Clark, and Production Assistant, Minju Kim, interviewed the immigrant students. Green Card Voices also contracted with Media Active to film the interviews and take the authors' portraits. Media Active is a youth-produced media production studio that provides teens and young adults with opportunities to gain valuable real-world job training and experience by creating professional-quality media products. The beautiful photographs and raw video footage are credited to David Buchanan, Dominica Asberry-Lindquist, and Ahxuen Ybarra.

We would also like to thank the GCV team: Shiney Her, Graphic Designer, who designed the interior of the book; Minju Kim, Video Editor, who worked with the student authors to transform raw video footage into compelling digital narratives; Jessie Lee-Bauder, Program Associate, who coordinated and supervised UW-Madison volunteers as well as the College Possible Milwaukee coaches, and assisted in editorial and promotional work throughout the book process; and our volunteer, Anna Boyer, who transcribed six Madison stories. Additionally, we thank Zaynab Abdi, Immigrant and Refugee Youth Ambassador, who came to Madison and Milwaukee to meet with each author in this volume to speak about various topics including her immigrant experience, as well as her role both as an author in the first GCV book and as a Malala Fund Delegate. We extend deep gratitude to Dr. Tea Rozman-Clark, GCV Co-Founder and Executive Director, whose vision and leadership allowed for the whole project to run smoothly. And finally, we thank the Board of Directors for supporting us in bringing Green Card Voices to Wisconsin. After developing a wonderful partnership with our collaborators in Fargo, North Dakota, as well as a lasting impact in the area, we are so excited to collaborate with our neighbor to the east, solidifying our presence and deepening our impact throughout the Midwest.

Beyond the above mentioned individuals and institutions, we would like to thank the Kennesaw State University English Department who continues to support Green Card Voices by providing editorial and writing support. Dr. Kim Haimes-Korn included the project in her upper level writing course and Dr. Lara Smith-Sitton in her role as the department's Director of Community Engagement supervised the final editorial work and glossary. Their process included review and copyediting of the essays by undergraduate students and a graduate student editorial team from the Master in Professional Writing program, followed by a close, final edit of the entire book by Dr. Smith-Sitton. Undergraduate editors included: Lauren Chiari, Catherine Darkwa, Himie Freeman, Holden Fromayan, Natalie Fuqua, Emily Jobe, Makayla Lenior, Cameron Meier, Kaitlin Perkins, John White, and Sam Wightman. Graduate students editors included: Courtney Bradford (co-lead editorial assistant), Willie Lawson, (co-lead editorial assistant), and Pearlie Harris as well as Emily Jobe, who was instrumental in fact-checking and organizing the glossary definitions before the editorial team and Dr. Lara Smith-Sitton finalized them. Upon completion of the editing process, Dr. Smith-Sitton wrote: "This is a powerful, powerful collection. We all paused and stepped away sometimes while editing. Tough stories from some strong, courageous, resilient young men and women."

Special thanks to our foreword author, Oscar Mireles, who prefaced these young people's stories with reflections of his own, sharing his story and his family's history. Oscar is the two-term Poet Laureate of Madison, Wisconsin, and the Executive Director of Omega School, an adult education institution. During his time there, Oscar has helped over 3,000 young adults secure their GED/HSED credentials. Oscar is also the force behind the three part anthology series, I Didn't Know There Were Latinos in Wisconsin, and is an instrumental community leader and builder in Madison, working to support emerging writers and amplify underrepresented voices.

For the first time ever, we are working with a national distributor, Consortium (Ingram), who will help us increase our access to schools, libraries, and individuals across Wisconsin as well as across the country, expanding our reach and allowing thousands of people to learn and grow through this book. We thank them for believing in us and going on this journey with us.

Thank you to Veronica Quillien, who designed the study guide and who is also the lead author of Voices of Immigrant Storytelling: Teaching Guide for Middle and High Schools. She is a first-generation immigrant and a PhD student in the Curriculum and Instruction Department at the University of Minnesota. We thank her for her expertise.

We are so grateful to Vianca Fuster of Radio Milwaukee, Annyssa Johnson of the Milwaukee Journal Sentinel, Negassi Tesfamichael of the Capital Times, Jenny Peek of Ithsmus and the Wisconsin Muslim Journal for seeing the value in these students' words and covering this project—thank you for amplifying our work!

A huge thank you to Latino Arts, Inc. for partnering with us to host our book launch celebration in Milwaukee. Elizabeth Tryon, Assistant Director of UW-Madison's Community Engaged Scholarship, was essential in securing space at the university for a Madison book launch. These partnerships ensured that the student authors could celebrate their achievements and be publicly recognized.

Thanks to our funders—from individuals who raised money via Facebook birthday fundraisers to major gift donors. Many people and organizations like College Possible National and Madison Public Schools also supported us by pre-ordering the book. Without you this publication would not have been possible!

Thanks to all of our board members present—Luis Versalles, Leslie Rapp, George C. Maxwell, Ruben Hidalgo, Gregory Eagan IV, Debjyoti Dwivedy, Mahlet Aschenaki, Richard Benton, Jane Berg Reidell, Shukri Hassan, Lara Smith-Sitton, and Andrew Gordon—as well as to all of our board members past— Jessica Cordova Kramer, Johan Eriksson, Masami Suga, Miguel Ramos, Hibo Abdi, Tara Kennedy, Veronica Quillien, Dana Boyle, Katie Murphy-Olsen, Jane Graupman, Ali Alizadeh, Laura Danielson, Jeff Corn, Ruhel Islam, Angela Eifert, Matt Kim, and Kathy Seipp—and all others who have helped our mission along the way.

Finally, and most personally, we would like to thank our spouses, children, families, and friends for helping each of us put our passion to use for the betterment of society.

With the above support, Green Card Voices is truly able to realize its mission of using the art of storytelling to build bridges between immigrants and their communities by sharing first-hand immigration stories of foreign-born Americans. Our aim is to help the collective us in the US see each "wave of immigrants" as individuals with assets and strengths that make this country remarkable.

Green Card Voices Team

Introduction

In our current political and cultural climate, dominant narratives of hate, fear, and xenophobia often shape the dialogue surrounding immigration to the US. Since 2013, Green Card Voices has been filling the need for the authentic, first person narratives of America's immigrants and refugees, building bridges among immigrants and their communities through the art of storytelling. Our organization's programs are designed to foster empathy and inclusive communities for all by acting as a counterweight to the negative rhetoric and stereotypes about contemporary immigration. Our work is needed now more than ever, and it reminds us that the American landscape and culture since its founding has always been rich due to the mixture of races, ethnicities, and cultures that together create a stronger and more vibrant country. We also pause here to acknowledge the Native Americans whose land we now inhabit and the descendants of Africans who were forcibly brought here.

According to the US Census Bureau, an estimated 13.4% of our population, or 43.2 million individuals, were not born in the US. Immigration to the US is increasing—by 2050, one in five Americans will be an immigrant. This is not unusual, as the US has enjoyed similar periods where immigration strengthened our country through cultural growth and development. There is no other country in the world where immigration has represented such a large portion of the overall population.[1]

Green Card Voices and our collaborators work every day to uplift stories of immigrants, refugees, and their families in order for all to be welcomed here. We do this through our online video platform, book collections, teaching guides, traveling exhibits, and storyteller panels at schools, libraries, and conferences.

This book will introduce you to young people living in the crossroads of the immigration debate, who live and grow and plan for their futures even as an uncertain political climate and negative immigration rhetoric dominates our media, our politics, and, sometimes, our dinner table conversations. Young authors share their hopes and dreams, which so often include their desires to make the US a better place for all. Their aspirations should remind us of the achievements of earlier immigrants whose significant con-

1. Pew Hispanic Trends Project (2013). U.S. Immigration Population Trends.

tributions shaped our country.

Green Card Youth Voices: Immigration Stories from Madison and Milwaukee High Schools is Green Card Voices' fifth anthology of essays written by young immigrants. The first book, based in Minneapolis, Minnesota, was published in May 2016 and received a Gold Medal Award from the Moonbeam Children's Book Awards. That collection serves as the template for our success. We recorded an additional 111 stories from young people in Fargo, North Dakota; St. Paul, Minnesota; and Atlanta, Georgia, compiling three additional anthologies based in each of these cities. With *Green Card Youth Voices: Immigration Stories from Madison and Milwaukee High Schools*, we've travelled to Minnesota's eastern neighbor and worked to share more diverse stories of immigrants and refugees who have moved to the Midwest.

Wisconsin has welcomed many different immigrant groups over the years. In the nineteenth century, many immigrants came from Germany, Scandinavia, and other parts of Europe. A steady source of immigrants throughout the state's history also came from Canada. Since the 1970s, several increasingly large phases of immigration from Mexico and other nations around Latin America have left imprints around the state, particularly in Milwaukee and the dairy and farming industries in more rural areas.[2] Nationally, over 50% of workers in the dairy industry are immigrants, and Wisconsin is the second largest producer of milk in the country. Much has been written about this immigrant group, who are rapidly transforming the face of the dairy industry in the state.[3]

In recent decades, immigrants and refugees from Asia have also increasingly made Wisconsin their home. Beginning in 1976, Hmong refugees fleeing war and persecution for fighting with American troops in Vietnam and Laos began resettling in the US. Since this time, Wisconsin's Hmong population has grown to be the third largest in the US, following California and Minnesota. Despite having been a part of the larger Wisconsin community for over forty years, many Hmong communities still face racialized stereotypes and prejudices. Nonetheless, resiliency thrives in these communities. According to *Wisconsin's Hmong Population*, Wisconsin's Hmong communities have seen tremendous economic growth; for example, "from 1990 to 2000, the percent of Hmong living in owner-occupied homes increased

2. Hall, D.J., Vetterkind, R. (2017, October). Why Immigrant Workers Became The Backbone Of Wisconsin's Dairy Business. Wisconsin Center for Investigative Journalism WisContext. Retrieved from www.wiscontext.org/wisconsins-diverse-waves-immigration
3. WisContext. (2019). Series: Wisconsin's Diverse Waves Of Immigration. Retrieved from www.wiscontext.org/why-immigrant-workers-became-backbone-wisconsins-dairy-business

from 9.9% to 48.2%. In contrast, among the total Wisconsin population, this percentage only increased from 66.7% to 68.4%."[4]

Wisconsin has a rich and diverse immigration history that continues to shape the region and evolve despite recent restrictions that have dramatically limited the number of immigrants and refugees admitted to Wisconsin . . . as well as to the US as a whole. According to the Refugee Processing Center, only 22,491 refugees were resettled in 2018, which is a significant 74% decrease from the 84,994 refugees resettled in the US in 2016. The effects of these restrictions were mirrored in Wisconsin, where 472 refugees were resettled in 2018, down 75% from the 1,877 refugees who made the state their home in 2016.[5]

Although the number of displaced people around the world has reached unprecedented levels, nationwide restrictions on refugee resettlement meant that in 2018, Wisconsin welcomed the lowest number of refugees in a decade. The number of countries of origin represented by recent refugees is also declining with refugees from Myanmar and the Democratic Republic of the Congo accounting for nearly all resettlements. As of 2018, Milwaukee was home to nearly 70% of these new refugee arrivals in Wisconsin.[6]

Many find it surprising that Milwaukee is also home to the largest Rohingya community in the US, with over 600 Rohingya families living in the city. While many refugees from Myanmar are Karen, a growing number are also Rohingya, a majority-Muslim ethnic group from Myanmar. The Rohingya people have been denied citizenship in Myanmar since 1982, and fled escalating violence ever since. The persecution of the Rohingya people follow patterns of ethnic cleansing that have emerged in the country.[7] Many Rohingya refugees settling in Wisconsin left Myanmar in the 1990s lived in Malaysia, where they continued to be subjected to limited rights before being able to come to the US.[8] On December 13, 2018, the US House of Representatives overwhelmingly passed a resolution declaring that the crimes com-

4. Karon, J., Long, D. Veroff D. (2003, August). Wisconsin's Hmong Population: Census 2000 Population and Other Demographic Trends. University of Wisconsin Extension & Applied Population Laboratory. Retrieved from https://apl.wisc.edu/publications/HmongChartbook.pdf

5. Refugee Processing Center. (2019). Admissions & Arrivals — Refugee Processing Center. Retrieved from http://www.wrapsnet.org/admissions-and-arrivals.

6. Cushman, W. (2019, January). Refugee Arrivals To Wisconsin, U.S. Plunge For Second Consecutive Year. WisContext. Retrieved from www.wiscontext.org/refugee-arrivals-wisconsin-us-plunge-second-consecutive-year

7. UN Women. (2018, August). Crisis Update: Nearly One Million Rohingya Refugees are in Bangladesh Now. Retrieved from www.unwomen.org/en/news/stories/2018/8/feature-rohingya-humanitarian-update

8. Holland, R. (2018, February). How Two Midwest Cities are Handling Rohingya Resettlement. Pacifics Standard. Retrieved from https://psmag.com/social-justice/how-two-midwest-cities-are-handling-rohingya-resettlement

mitted by Myanmar's security forces against Rohingya Muslims constitute genocide.[9]

Madison and Milwaukee are respectively the capital and the largest city in Wisconsin, and each has a rich and growing immigrant population. According to the University of Wisconsin Applied Population Lab, Wisconsin's immigrant communities have grown by over 130% since the early 1990s. Milwaukee County's population is made up of 30% immigrants.

The high schools we chose for this book shared similar characteristics: all have a high percentage of immigrant students, and as a group, they reflect broader immigration trends in Wisconsin. While the students featured in each of the Green Card Voices' earlier books all lived in the same city and attended the same high school (except in Atlanta where students attended three different schools), this volume includes students who attend two separate schools in two different Wisconsin cities. This approach allows for the reader to gain an understanding of immigrant stories within a state but beyond just one city.

As of 2019, James Madison Memorial High School in Madison had nearly 2,000 students—194 of whom were born outside the US. Of these students, 121 were English Language Learners and many had successfully reached proficiency during their K–12 school period. Mexico and Honduras are the most common countries where students were born outside the US, although 42 additional countries are also represented.

Casimir Pulaski High School in Milwaukee had 850 students in 2019—15% of whom were Asian, 39% of whom were African-American/Black, 41% of whom were Hispanic/Latino, and 5% of whom were White. 40% of Pulaski High School's students were English Language Learners. In August of 2018 Pulaski High School became a fully authorized International Baccalaureate World School (IB) offering the Middle Years Program to students in ninth and tenth grades. According to the IB, this program encourages students to make practical connections between their studies and the real world.[10] Pulaski is also currently a candidate school for the Diploma and Career Programs. If and when this is authorized, all students will have an opportunity to pursue a four-year IB high school education.

The authors in the Madison and Milwaukee book represent a range of experiences and backgrounds, including new-arrivals and graduating se-

9. Hansler, J. (2018, December). House Says Myanmar Crimes Against Rohingya are Genocide. CNN. Retrieved from www.cnn.com/2018/12/13/politics/house-resolution-myanmar-genocide/index.html
10. Iborganization. (2019). "Education Programmes." International Baccalaureate®. Retrieved from www.ibo.org/programmes/

niors, refugees and green card holders. Several were even born in the US but were raised in the countries from which their parents migrated. They are the emerging scientists, doctors, business owners, elected officials, and community leaders that will shape the Madison and Milwaukee landscape as well as the American Midwest for the foreseeable future. These young people are wise beyond their years, and their communities will greatly benefit from their shared experiences, talents and insights.

The process of creating this book was specifically designed to meet the needs of the young immigrants. Many have had limited or interrupted educations. For these reasons, we recorded the authors speaking their stories before we ever approached the written page. Then, in the spirit of the educational and civic engagement opportunities created by our work, we continued the tradition of community engagement by partnering with area universities, professors, and students to create community-writing and service learning experiences that expand the reach of these stories. In line with this, the narratives were transcribed by a group of student editors from the University of Wisconsin-Madison, as well as College Possible Milwaukee coaches, who then worked with the immigrant authors to develop and refine their essays while retaining each student's unique voice. A group of English Department students at Kennesaw State University in Georgia also served as copyeditors and produced the glossary. Along every step of the way, the immigrant authors were in control of their narratives, and what you read within these pages and watch in the videos reflects immense bravery.

Bravery is what is required to share these stories. This book comes forward in challenging times for immigrants in the US. In 2017 and today, different segments from the immigrant community face unique challenges: the banning of citizens from eight countries, most of which are majority-Muslim, from entering the US; reducing refugee admissions to the lowest levels since the creation of the resettlement program in 1980; and canceling the Deferred Action for Childhood Arrivals (DACA) program, affecting 800,000 immigrants brought to the US as minor children. Following the enactment of a zero-tolerance immigration policy in 2018 by the US Justice Department, over 2,500 children were separated from their parents.[11] Separated children were sent to 121 different detention or care centers in seventeen states throughout the country, often hundreds or thousands of miles away

11. Ballotpedia. (2019). Timeline of Federal Policy on Immigration, 2017-2020. Ballotpedia. Retrieved from https://ballotpedia.org/Timeline_of_federal_policy_on_immigration,_2017-2020#March_20.2C_2018:_Trump_claims_sanctuary_cities_harbor_criminals

from where their parents were held.[12] The summer of 2019 saw unprecedented, deadly overcrowding at detention facilities, with centers holding migrants and asylum seekers at rates over seven times their capacity. Overcrowding and a subsequent lack of space, basic toiletries, or food rations exacerbated dangerously unhygienic conditions. As of June 2019, over 2,500 children were being detained at the border, and at least six children died in custody between September and June.[13]

Now more than ever, Green Card Voices and other organizations that help share the stories of immigrants have a role to play to expand our understanding of the immigrant experience and to highlight the contributions made by this powerful community. To uphold our country's founding principles of liberty, justice, equality, and dignity for all, we must remember that with diverse newcomers comes growth and opportunity.

We hope that this book inspires a spirit of openness and inclusion that has been the cornerstone of our country. We believe sharing stories is a powerful tool that can help us reach the goal of a fully integrated and compassionate society. Stories not only empower the teller, whose life experiences and unique contributions become valuable and validated through sharing, but they also educate the broader public and help us see how we all share the experience of being human. We hope you will be as moved as we are by the stories in this book. These writers came to the US, as generations have before, seeking a place where they could breathe the free air, live life with dignity, and enjoy equal justice under the law. It is our job to build a society of compassion and hope, worthy to be the garden in which their treasured dreams can grow. We hope that reading about the memories, realities, and hopes of these thirty young people will inspire you. Their courage shows that the future of Wisconsin—and indeed of the United States of America itself—is in good hands.

Dr. Tea Rozman Clark   Jessie Lee-Bauder
Green Card Voices   Green Card Voices

---

12. American Civil Liberties Union. (2019). Family Separation by the Numbers. Retrived from www.aclu.org/issues/immigrants-rights/immigrants-rights-and-detention/family-separation.
13. Flynn, Meagan. (2019, June). "Attorneys Seek Emergency Court Order to End 'Health and Welfare Crisis' in Migrant Detention Centers." The Washington Post, WP Company. Retrived from www.washingtonpost.com/nation/2019/06/27/attorneys-seek-emergency-court-order-end-health-welfare-crisis-migrant-detention-centers/?utm_term=.27e3d8d0f78f

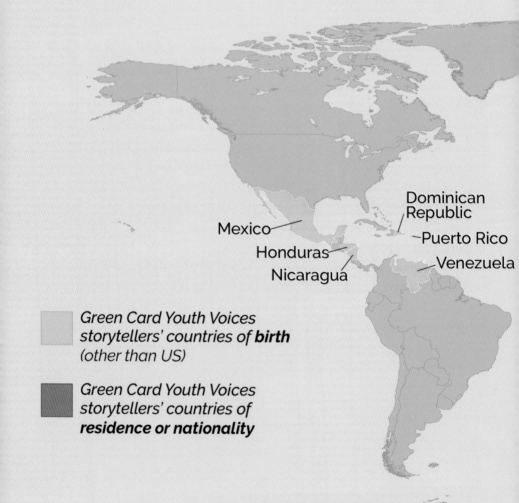

Mexico

Dominican
Republic

Puerto Rico

Honduras

Venezuela

Nicaragua

Green Card Youth Voices
*storytellers' countries of **birth***
(other than US)

Green Card Youth Voices
storytellers' countries of
residence or nationality

World Map

Syria
Iraq
Pakistan
Nepal
Laos
India
Vietnam
Thailand
Ethiopia
Somalia
Myanmar
(Burma)
Malaysia
Ghana
Kenya

Personal Essays

Stephanie Salgado

From: Tegucigalpa, Honduras
Current City: Madison, WI

"IT DOES NOT MATTER WHAT TYPE OF PEOPLE BELITTLE YOU BUT INSTEAD WHAT YOU DO TO CHANGE IT. WHEN YOU COME HERE AND YOU REALIZE YOU ARE A MINORITY, YOU KIND OF EMBRACE IT. THAT'S REALLY THE BEAUTY OF WHAT BEING AN IMMIGRANT HERE IS."

During my fourteen years of life in Honduras, I realized that the privilege my dad and my mom had in going to college and having good jobs allowed them to isolate me and my sister from what Honduras really was. At the time it was a really beautiful country, but as time passed, security got really under-valued and many people started stirring up violence due to the corruption in politics. Even though we were really well taken care of—I would even argue spoiled—we could not live there. When my family left, I recalled a lot of beau-tiful moments that were stripped from us because we desired a better future.

In Honduras, I would wake up in the room I shared with my sister. I would go to school around 7 a.m., which was really early compared to the US. Then I would be in school all the way up until 4 p.m. Despite the fact that volleyball was the only sport for girls, I decided to try out for basketball. We couldn't compete because it was co-ed. I also remember I couldn't choose my classes or the peers I could be with. It was really disappointing that you would always converse with the same people having the same idea. After school I would go home and normally do my homework if my parents told me to, but I didn't really have an interest in school. I just thought teachers made you memo-rize books and terms, which didn't really encourage me to learn unfortunately.

On the weekends I would say we were happy and warm because the family would always be reunited. On Saturday we'd go to mass and then have Chinese food at my grandma's house. Everyone always brought more and more food afterwards, too. I know we gained a lot of weight because of it. Still, I really liked having my family reunite to talk about life and simply be together.

On spring break my entire family would always go to a beach in Omoa because it was only a two-hour drive. I remember that it was so hot! As the years passed, I realized how much trash was brought in by the ocean. That's when I started realizing how we were affecting the environment, and it built up my awareness. For birthdays people would bring gifts, but not a lot of them, and you just wanted to spend time with your family. Thanksgiving is not really a holiday there, but we had family in the United States and thus knew what it was. Even though my mom called it turkey, we really ate chicken. At Christmas me and my cousins would doubt the legitimacy of a Santa who was dark-skinned and spoke Spanish because we knew Santa generally looked Caucasian. Still, I just happily remember all those memories.

I had no idea my parents planned to leave Honduras. The day I found out, I had already come back from school. I think I had my homework done—but probably not—when my parents came home. They said, "We have to talk you," and brought my sister and I to the room, sat down, and stared at us. My sister and I thought, "Oh my gosh!" We were looking at each other like what did you do this time? Then my dad said, "I have completed twenty years working in the US Embassy, and I have the opportunity to ask for residence for us as a family to move to the United States." Immediately, I just stared and said, "What an amazing opportunity!"

I thought it would be such an eye-opening experience even though I had to leave everything behind, including my identity. Some Hondurans in America ask if I am ashamed to be Honduran because they say we are not viewed as a trustworthy people, but I would always respond, "It does not matter what type of people belittle you but instead what you do to change it." When you come here and you realize you are a minority, you kind of embrace it. That's really the beauty of what being an immigrant here is.

Before we moved we sold our cars, our stuff, and our clothes. At the end we only had two t-shirts and a pair of pants. It was really a struggle because we had to pack our whole lifetime into a forty-pound luggage. We couldn't bring a lot of clothes or memories. It was pretty sad, but I'm still grateful for it.

The day we left Honduras, we woke up at 4:00 a.m. We got to the airport at 6:00 a.m. I remember it was not my first time riding in an airplane, but it was definitely the first ride that was just one way. I knew we were not coming back, so it was not a vacation. I was aware about the fact that we were not going to buy a lot of stuff until we had more stability.

We traveled from Tegucigalpa to Chicago. My aunt picked us up in a car. All the way back there, I asked her things like, "Is there such a thing called a dishwasher here?" I thought dishwashers were incredible since I had to wash dishes by hand on a daily basis in Honduras. I also told her I was so excited to try out new sports. They have female sports here—more than just volleyball! Moreover, I was excited I could choose my classes and who I would hang out with. Because of that, I was really excited all the way there!

When I first came to Madison, I noticed that there were no fences around the houses. I saw no security, no guards, no people wandering around with their dogs trying to protect their household or their belongings. They had their garages open, which just seemed so weird. I also remember drinking from the water fountain and thinking that this was not how you drink water. In Honduras you had to buy water first because it was privatized.

Initially I went to Toki Middle School because I had yet to finish eighth grade. When they came in, they said, "How old are you?" I said, "Well, I was born September 1, 2001." Then they said, "You're good to go to high school." I did not even complete an entrance test to see where I was at, which was pretty hard. My whole family was really hoping for me to transition at the middle school first to improve my English and then go to high school because they knew that you start preparing to apply for college there.

So, I went into freshman year, and it was really hard. Even though I took algebra and geometry in Honduras, they said I had to retake it. I was really struggling to understand the methods because some methods are taught differently in Honduras. In algebra it was so weird to see my teacher solve problems a different way from what I was taught, and I didn't always understand it. I also saw how some kids would disrespect teachers, which is such an infamous thing to do in Honduras. You would get sent to the dean, and that would be the end of your world—that was the scariest part of school.

I also saw how we had to be so dependent and, at the same time, independent—dependent in the sense that we depended on our parents to give us food, money for lunch, and know where we were going next year for college. Unfortunately, my parents failed to guide me in this process because they were not knowledgeable of the American system. They did not know what the ACT was or about applying for colleges.

In contrast to Honduras, I was independent here in the sense that I got to choose my classes. I could choose if I wanted to do easy classes, which my parents wanted me to do, but I said no because I really want to challenge myself. I know it will affect my GPA, but I'm not here to memorize. I started to realize that school is where we really start learning how to connect what we learn to the future and how to use this information to make a better outcome. I also saw how differently the students dressed. We had uniforms in Honduras, but here you can express yourself. You can go out and say that you're part of the LGBT community, which was such a no-no thing in our Catholic school. It was not talked about. You could not dye your hair; you could not wear makeup; you could not have a relationship. In Honduras it was like being incarcerated in a box. Here I felt like I was released into a new world with new opportunities.

At Memorial I started doing a lot more clubs: forensics, drama, Women's Club, AVID Student Council, and Book Club. I founded the Green Club to promote environmental awareness. For Green Club and Book Club, I'm a coordinator. In Book Club, we read very analytical books that are very challenging morally. We talk about a lot of different books, and we love it. I was involved in Women's Club and AVID Student Council, which is a club where students make decisions about AVID, a college preparatory class. It's meant to close the achievement gap for students of color and those who are otherwise disadvantaged. Throughout high school I did soccer, which was finally open to girls, tried out for basketball, and participated in cross-country for the first time. Soccer was really special for me because I got to meet people and understand how their experiences were different from mine. I also realized that people would go out to restaurants all the time, which was something you would only do for your birthday or special events back in Honduras. Yet, despite a lot of culture shock, I realized that I now understand where they are coming from and why they are coming from a different perspective. That means I have no right to judge anybody on what they think about my country or my background because they were raised differently here.

I'm also involved in Scholars of Color whose members are people of color doing AP or honors classes and don't feel really represented there, which is something I experienced. My sophomore year, when I went to AP World, I saw that nobody looked like me. It was so intimidating; I thought I was not ready. It was hard. At the end of the year, my teacher told me, "I don't think you're going to pass the AP test because your English is not at the same level as the other students. It would be really hard for you to write an essay in forty-five minutes." But in the end I went there, took it, and got a three, which is a passing grade. I was so excited and so happy. I realized that a grade, even though it doesn't define you, can tell you that your work will pay off.

This experience has made me want to be a model—not in the sense of shopping or clothes—but a role model for young girls. Once I realized that there's a lot of people that look like me going through the same thing, I wanted to help others who don't feel represented to realize that, even if your parents are not telling you to challenge yourself, do it anyway. Even if they're not telling you to get into a certain college to be really proud of you, do it anyway. I really hope that the readers of this book will realize that there are people out there that look like you, and that you can do this regardless of your background.

Currently I'm in my senior year. I really started narrowing down the activities I was doing to prepare for college. I got into all seven colleges I applied for. I'm happy to announce I will be attending UW–Madison next year.

As of now I'm just working and trying to earn money for college because I don't think my parents have realized that college is expensive, especially if you extend your four years and attend law school. I really want to pursue a career in environmental science because I want to change the world. That way I'm not only contributing to the environment here in the United States but also in Honduras. I want to let them know about the dangers of palm oil and monoculture. I want to change the stereotypes around race and affluence, which is a really big problem here in the United States. That's why I'm going to the University of Wisconsin–Madison to pursue a career in environmental science. Then I want to go to law school and start talking to politicians. I intend to ask them, "What are your long-term plans about impacting our environment?"

Still, despite the fact that I sound like a really well-rounded student, being too involved was very detrimental to my mental health. If you're looking at this and you're a high school student, just narrow it down and do the things you're passionate about—not just because someone else is doing it and you think that's going to help you get into college. If you aren't passionate about it, then don't do it. Just narrow down your choices—take the classes you want and just be happy and enjoy life.

VIDEO LINKS

greencardvoices.org/speakers/stephanie-salgado

ASIA

Châu Thành,
Vietnam

Vy Luong

From: Châu Thành, Vietnam
Current City: Madison, WI

"MY MOM WAS VERY SERIOUS ABOUT SCHOOL BECAUSE SHE NEVER ACTUALLY GOT TO GO INTO COLLEGE BECAUSE SHE'S HALF AMERICAN. MY GRANDFATHER IS AMERICAN, AND HE FOUGHT IN THE VIETNAM WAR. THERE WAS DISCRIMINATION AGAINST HER GOING TO COLLEGE AT THE TIME."

I was born in Châu Thành District in Tiền Giang Province, Vietnam. That is a small town, about five hundred people, down south of Ho Chi Minh City. I lived in a small house with my grandmother, my mom, my younger brother, and a few cousins. The house was in the back of a middle school and next to a church. It was in front of a police station and nearby a market. Everything was just really packed together. Living conditions before my brother was born were a little tough. It was very unsanitary. The house was very old; it was starting to crumble down, and we didn't have a toilet. We had to go in the bushes behind the house. My mom was the only source of income at the time, so we kind of had to eat the same thing every day, which was rice and potatoes pretty much. My younger brother was born roughly five, almost six years after I was born. That was when my cousins started a cafe in the back of the house to sell coffee to the policemen because it's by a police station. By then, we started to have a little more income, and we got the house rebuilt to be a little stronger and sturdier, and we got a toilet installed, so from there the living condition had been improved a little bit. For as long as I can remember, I've always had friends and family on my side, clothes on my back, and a roof over my head.

School was great. The building was right in front of my house because I live in an area where it's packed with everything. I took English, science, math, Vietnamese, of course, and music because it was also required. My mom was very serious about school because she never actually got to go into college because she's half American. My grandfather is American, and he fought in the Vietnam War. There was discrimination against her going to college at the time. They never openly said that she was not allowed to, but they made it very difficult to go beyond high school. They have to do testing to get into university, and she actually never passed the tests. She wants me to go all the way, so she takes school very seriously. In my free time, I spent a lot of time in my church—the house is right next to a church, so I spent a lot of time there after school and on the weekends. I served there. I spent a lot of time with the priest. My other friends also spent time in the church a lot. I also took Tae Kwon Do classes; if I was not at Tae Kwon Do classes, I would be in church.

At the beginning of sixth grade, I was informed that I was going to go to the US to reunite with my grandfather. At the time I didn't really know how to process it because they never mentioned me having a grandfather on my mom's side before. It was just all new information, so I didn't really think too deep into it, but my grandfather is an American that served in the Vietnam War. He met my grandmother in Vietnam, and had my mom in 1969, which is near the end of the war in 1975. After the war was over, he returned to the US, and they kind of lost contact for almost forty years. A mutual friend of my grandparents came back to Vietnam to visit and unintentionally met my grandmother. After he returned back to the US, he got us reconnected with my grandfather. The paperwork process started very soon right after he came back because now we know that my grandfather's still alive, and he knows that we're still alive, so we got the paperwork started to have that reunion.

I didn't really know how to process the information at the time. My original impression of America was that everybody would be rich and can freely express themselves. I grew up with the impression that if you are in America, you are happier than anywhere else. I did not have a lot of knowledge about America.

One day my mom suddenly told me that we will be going on a plane to go to America. I didn't realize I was going to go to America so soon. After we got our visas, we only had four months to pack to restart our whole lives. I just left it to my family to decide what to pack. I actually went to school all the way until the day before we were supposed to take off to fly to the US. It was very emotional for me during the last day of school. All of my friends were crying; I was also crying. I didn't know how my life was going to be in the US, but I knew that I wouldn't have the same friends again. I knew I wouldn't have all the time I spent in church with them. I had to leave behind my family and my cousins. I just knew it was going to be bittersweet.

The process of getting the visa was very difficult. We had to go to the US consulate in Ho Chi Minh City to be interviewed to make sure that my mom and my grandfather were actually biologically related. Every time we had to rent a car to go to Ho Chi Minh City, and it was very expensive because we didn't have that source of income, and my mom would get car sick because it's a very long car ride from where I lived. We had to get vaccinated, and my mom had some problems with her health records, so we had to get that cleared up. The process was really long and tiring for me, but my mom was very passionate about it because I knew she was eagerly wanting to see her father again. It was real heartwarming to see the reunion after all that process.

I went with my brother, mom, and my grandmother to the airport. I don't think my brother realized what was happening at the time. There were never any problems with him on the plane or anything. We took off in Ho Chi Minh City on the November 14, 2012, and it was 3:00 in the morning. We took off, and we were planning to go all the way to Los Angeles in one trip, but the plane had to make an emergency landing in Alaska, so we had to spend the night there. It was very scary because I didn't know what to expect at that moment—nobody in our family did, so to have that as the first thing that ever happened on the journey was very faith-shaking. We were all very afraid of what was going to happen in the future. But we spent a night there in Alaska, and in the morning we took off to go to Los Angeles. It had been two days since we left Vietnam already. After Los Angeles we took off again and went straight to Milwaukee. It was November 17, 2012. We landed at approximately 8:00 p.m.

When we first came out the gate, Jim, who was a friend of my family that helped reconnect my grandfather and my grandmother in Vietnam, handed us an American flag. When we stepped out the gate, we saw Santa Claus or a person dressed as a Santa Claus. We took a picture together. Of course in the picture there was my brother, me and my mom, and my grandma on the side as well. We saw Santa Claus for the first time. It was pretty cool.

We went out to eat afterwards. There was a Vietnamese restaurant nearby, so we went there to have some soup, and then we drove to Madison to our apartment where our grandfather was. He doesn't live with us, but he was there to wait for us.

My mom was the first to walk into the apartment, and my grandpa was there on his knees and was hugging my mom. She cried a little bit. I think he left Vietnam when she was like two or three years old. I think she knew she had a father, but she didn't remember much, so seeing him again after forty years was, I think, a little bit shocking and emotional. I didn't cry just because I was so tired. I hadn't slept in like two days. But seeing that was very rewarding, and at that moment, I knew that it was worth all the troubles before.

The first hour after I landed, it was very cold—it was freezing! I've never experienced that temperature before. And my lips . . . I just remember my lips were very dried and swollen. I hadn't slept in two days due to the jetlag, so I wasn't really paying attention much for the first few days. After the first week when I actually adapted enough, I realized that there's a lot more space here—it's not packed together like where I used to live in Vietnam.

For the first few months, we were just waiting to get our Green Cards and our Social Security cards and all that paperwork so I can start school. I just stayed in the house, and it was pretty boring at the time. My grandfather is married again, so he has a wife. They bought us the basics—utilities, towels, shampoo, and all that stuff, but we also received help from the Catholic Multi-cultural Center, which is within walking distance from where we used to live. They gave us beds, dishes, and all that, but apart from that, the house was pretty much empty at the time.

I started school roughly a month and a half after I landed in America. I did not speak any English. I knew like the basic stuff. I knew "hello" and "how are you" but I couldn't communicate. I couldn't talk to teachers or students at all. When we first started school, they did a little testing to test where I was standing in English. They put me in all the classes that other kids were taking. Besides math I couldn't do anything else but sit in the back of the class and just observe. There was one class where there was this bilingual teacher. She was helping us slowly learn vocabs and learn how to start a conversation. There was another teacher that would go to some classes with me, and he always had his iPad, and we would use Google Translate when I tried to understand something.

School was pretty tough at first. From middle school to the first two years of high school . . . it was very tough. The language barrier got me to experience bullying for the first time. The kids would just make fun of how I speak or how I present myself because I would always stand out as being a little different. I don't know what triggered the bullying, but I remember at times there were comments made and laughter, but I couldn't understand them at the moment, of course. I guess I could just feel it at the time that people didn't have very much of a nice opinion of me at the time.

The teachers were amazing. They always tried to be so encouraging, and they were willing to do everything to help me adapt more and get used to the language, so from that period of time for a few months I was just sitting in the back of the class silently until I was able to pick up some English and be able to process the concepts in class.

I want my story to let people know that you shouldn't be afraid of changes. As an immigrant, I started my life over in a new country, and I've had the experience of starting over in a new school, too. When I started high school at Madison West High School, I felt very comfortable with my surroundings in school and outside of school. That continued all the way to sophomore year. I felt like I was just going through the motions in my classes and with my friends. I didn't have to try so hard to receive good grades and fit in. At the end of sophomore year, I decided to transfer to a new high school. The main reason I transferred is that I wanted to challenge myself to improve my social skills, experience a new environment, and prove to myself that I can succeed in a new setting—just like I would need to do in college.

Junior year, I was approved to attend James Madison Memorial High School. At first I didn't know anybody in my classes. I made some friends through competitive cheerleading and track, but we weren't as close as I had been with the friends I'd made at West. Since I live across from the school, I would always go home for lunch due to the fact that I did not feel comfortable having lunch with new people. I had quite a few breakdowns during the beginning of the year, but I remembered the reason why I wanted to transfer in the first place. I started open myself up to peers around me by asking my classmates to have lunch together at the high school. Soon we would grow to be closer. I started to feel more comfortable. From there, I knew that I would start to blossom in school and socially.

In the time since I started my senior year, it has gotten a lot better. Now, I'm very close friends with my teammates in cheer and track. We always have lunch and participate in school functions together. This has made me much happier in school. Despite these changes, my friends from West and I still keep in touch. Instead of just feeling comfortable at West, now I feel more well-rounded because I know people from both schools. Transferring and adapting to a new school helped me to improve my social skills and to feel more comfortable in unfamiliar settings. If I were still attending West or did not step out of my comfort zone to meet new people, I would not have met the friends I have today nor would I have proven to myself that changes can help me grow as a person. Furthermore, attending Memorial does not alter the fact that I have spent two previous years at West and have friends there. In the same way, being an American does not alter my Vietnamese identity.

Life now is great. I am figuring myself out. I'm committed to attend UW–Madison in the fall of 2019. I intend to major in biology and possibly biochemistry in the College of Agricultural and Life Sciences. In June I am going to graduate with high honors, so that is something I look forward to. On the weekends I go to church. I also volunteer at in a youth group at church helping the freshmen learn about confirmation and as an altar server and a lay minister for the church. Faith has always been a big part of my life. It gives me a sense of security, and I feel like I am part of a universal family.

I don't try to fit in anymore. Before I knew any English and all the bullying happened, I always tried to fit in and be like every other kid to avoid the bullying, but after middle school I always tried to stand out a little bit, I guess you could say. I try to be myself more because, in my opinion, there's only one you, and you can be yourself best. That's how I believe in it. I always try to stand out and be a little bit different—from the way I dress or how I express myself. I want other people around me to know that it is okay to be different. I like to be different now.

My relationship with my mom is very strong now. Before this time we had like a culture clash while I was adapting to the American culture, and she was also very heavy on the Asian culture. When I was adapting to the culture after spending a few years here, I would start speaking a little English to her, and she would start to speak a little English back to me. Sometimes I would say "okay" to her, and she thinks that's a sign of disrespect. There were just little things like that that added up to her not fully understanding that I'm adapting to the culture. But, in her opinion, I was just trying to disrespect her. So, for a really long time we had this culture clash where we would always disagree over something that was very small and not significant. It was just little things that added up to a big clash. That happened for almost a year. We had that clash for a while, which was very tough for me because I felt like I couldn't fit into either culture without receiving backlash from either my family or the kids at school. But now she's very understanding. She's very supportive of me. It's always been us, so I'm grateful. At home we still speak Vietnamese, and we eat Vietnamese food almost every day.

We visited Vietnam during the summer between my freshman and sophomore years. My mom's goal is to have us visit every other year because our grandma is still over there, and she does not want us to forget our origins. For right now, I'm still grateful that I have got friends and family on my side, a roof over my head, clothes on my back, and, most importantly, public education.

First, I hope this story will let other immigrants know that it is okay to have turns and ups and downs in life, but it will always turn out in the end if you have dedication and you work hard. Secondly, I want to be a family physician because I want to be able to provide more than just medical help. I want to also connect with families because when I first came here our family physician was very supportive, and she got us to connect with the people that we needed. She helped me with school supplies. I want to be able to do that for families in the future. I also want to make myself a role model to help others see how to be more tolerant and to be a citizen of the world.

Now I have realized that you still have to earn the riches everybody in Vietnam assumed all Americans have, and people are still fighting for human rights for certain groups of people. I try to be a little more open-minded about social and political issues. I'm a very liberal person, but I also want to be open-minded to hear about conservative sides as well—not just closing myself up to being liberal but also trying to hear other people's sides. I'm trying to be more tolerant, and I'm trying to be more open-minded.

I've realized that my grandfather was also an immigrant. He immigrated here when he was five. He told me that he came to Canada first with his family, and then they migrated to Wisconsin. All happened when he was five years old, so immigration has always been a part of me.

VIDEO LINKS

greencardvoices.org/speakers/vy-luong

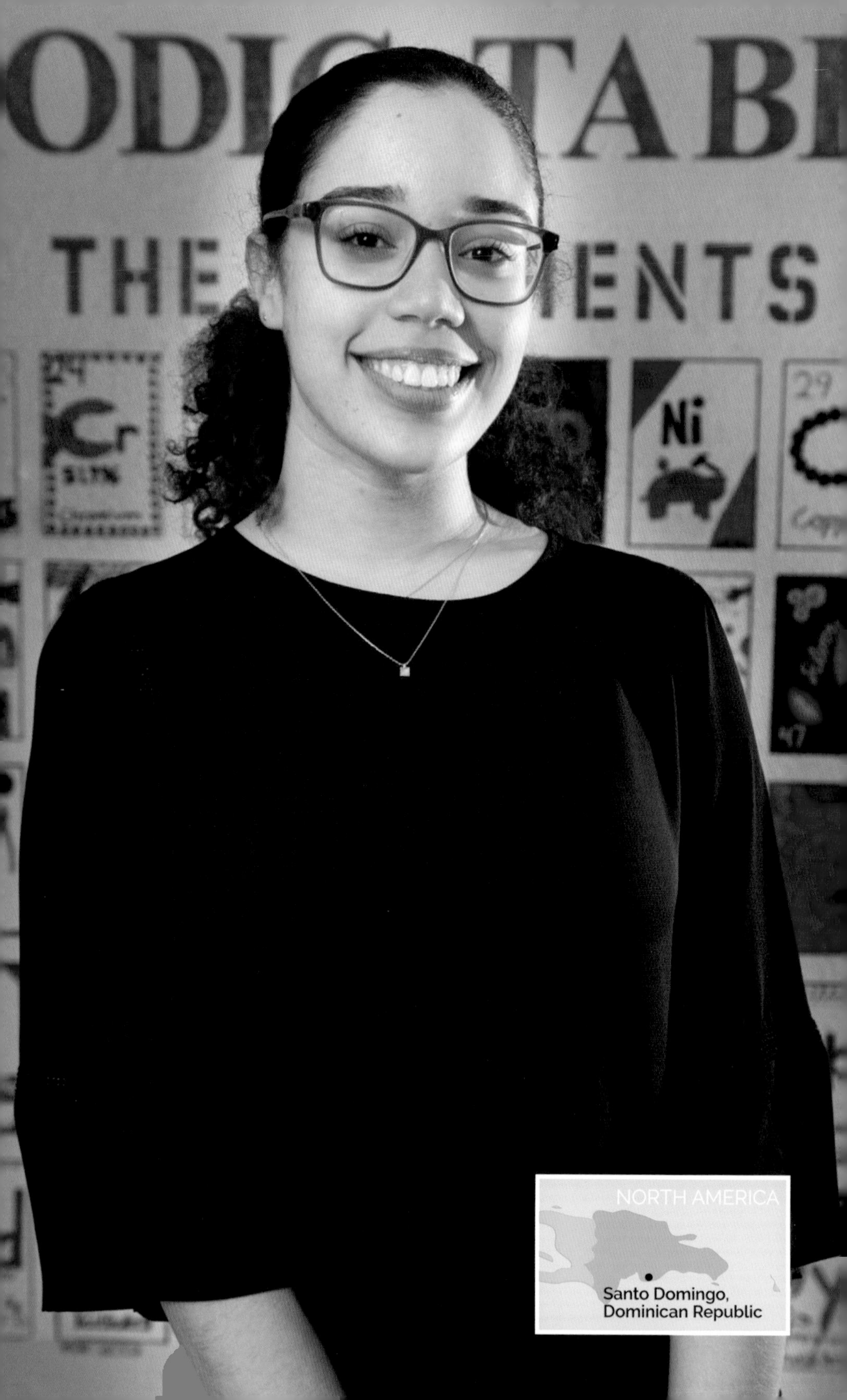
NORTH AMERICA
Santo Domingo,
Dominican Republic

Christine Encarnacion

Born: Paterson, NJ   **Raised:** Santo Domingo, Dominican Republic
Current City: Madison, WI

> "I REALLY WANT TO HELP INSPIRE OTHER MINORITIES TO GO INTO STEM, ESPECIALLY FEMALES SINCE IT'S SO INTIMIDATING BASED ON GENDER OR ETHNICITY OR RACE. IT'S HONESTLY REALLY HARD BECAUSE I FELT SO SCARED WHEN I FIRST GOT INTO IT."

I was born in Paterson, New Jersey. After a month of me being born, we went back to Dominican Republic, which is where my dad and mom were born, and that's where I was raised. Growing up on an island made me feel so lucky. I love the weather, the culture, the food, and the music. It made me feel so proud to be from the country. I remember waking up every day to the sound of bells from the church and getting ready for school and going to school to sing the national anthem, which is always something that I looked forward to.

I grew up with both of my parents, my brothers, my grandma, and my uncles. I lived right across from my grandma with just a strip of street that separated us, so I would visit her every single day. I also went to church every day of my life, so religion was very important to me growing up and is also something that I identify myself with when I consider myself a Dominican.

My life in Dominican Republic was one that I think shaped me into the person that I am now. I came from a very humble beginning. Even when we never had enough money, my parents never made me feel like I lacked anything. They always did everything for me to feel like I had the entire world. I remember one time, in our very tiny apartment, we had giant pieces of wood, and my dad and I made a rocket. We stacked the pieces of wood up in our hallway, and we sat on them and put hamper baskets over our heads like we were astronauts. That's one of the most memorable things that I know.

I remember my mom telling me there was a chance we might move to the United States, but it was never confirmed, so I never thought about it. I just thought it might not even happen. And then one day, my dad was already in the United States working for a year before we moved there. One day he sent me and my brothers brand new suitcases out of nowhere. I remember I had a tiny pink suitcase. I asked what the suitcase was for, and my mom said we were moving to America, and I remember I was screaming I was so excited.

I remember telling all my friends, all my teachers, that I was I going to learn English and that I was moving. The only places I knew in America were New York or Washington, so I told them I was moving to Washington. I was so excited to move. I remember my mom telling me that we were going to have to be away from my grandma and that we might just visit over the summer. Obviously, I was not ready for that, but it was still so exciting. Since I was only nine, there wasn't much I was giving up to come to the United States. I gave up my country and being able to go to high school there, but mostly I gave up seeing most of my family. Living with my grandma was the biggest thing I had to give up. Unfortunately, my grandma passed away in 2014, which was really hard. So in terms of going back to Dominican Republic, I hope to go before I go to college just to see her house again and my house and the church (since when I moved she built a new church). She was the pastor of the church that I went to, so I really want to go see that.

We ended up moving on Christmas day, so before we left, I remember we got my grandma a Christmas tree, and my grandma gave me a pink watch. She told me to be careful, and we went to the airport. I fell asleep the entire plane ride, but when I got off the plane, I saw snow for the first time. I remember always seeing snow on the TV, and it doesn't snow in Dominican Republic, so I was thinking, "What is this?" When I touched it and saw it dissolve in my hands and saw that it was cold, I thought it was just a weird feeling. I got there at nighttime, and it was Christmas, and it was really nice.

When I first moved to America, I moved to Pennsylvania, and I lived there for two years. My mom had a friend in Delaware, so we decided to move there cause we have a connection there. After living there for one year, we decided we would feel more comfortable in Pennsylvania. We moved back, and we lived there for about five or six years. I did my entire middle school there.

When we first were in Pennsylvania, my dad already had a rented house for us since he was already living there, so when I got there, I was so excited because it was much bigger than our apartment that we had in Dominican Republic. So then soon after settling in, which took like two months, I started school late. My class already knew that they were getting a foreign student. My teacher had asked my parents about things that I like, so they said sunflowers cause my grandma always had sunflowers and I love them, and they mentioned my favorite foods and everything. So when I got to school, I remember the kids drew sunflowers for me, which was so nice. They were all very interested in what my life was like and how it was going from another country, but I didn't speak English, so I was so nervous. I remember the first thing that I noticed was my curly hair: I had big long curly hair, and I was the only one that stood out. That's when I realized it's going to be so obvious that I'm so different. But I actually got very positive feedback from my classmates; they all loved to play with my hair and just ask me how I straighten it.

My freshman year of high school, I decided to join rugby cause all my friends were pressuring me to join. That was also very different. I was stepping outside of my comfort zone, which people should definitely do. I was so scared, but I ended up loving it, and I definitely want to continue playing rugby in college. Rugby is just so different from anything that I've ever done. When you tell someone that you play rugby, they're just so surprised. They're like, "You play rugby? That's so aggressive, it usually seems like a men's sport." But there's a ton of girls' rugby teams, especially here in Madison, that a lot of girls don't know about. I didn't even know about it—my friend told me about it, and that's why I ended up joining rugby. There are actually a lot of Latinas in rugby that I have played with on my team. There's five foreign girls, and we're proud of our diversity.

After living in Pennsylvania, my dad's company said that they needed someone to work in Mexico, and we honestly had no other option, so we all went to Mexico, which was so different. It was like the same experience all over again—meeting new people, different culture, different food, different what's socially acceptable. It was different morals and everything.

One of the things about moving to Mexico was that they didn't have rugby there. But one of my other passions was basketball, so I actually ended up starting a girls' basketball team. I had to get signatures from a lot of females, and then I was the manager for that, which was also really fun. It was encouraging to have support from the gym teacher who gave me the signature paper. I wanted to find something that girls would like to do. I remember girls would play basketball outside during lunchtime, and I would join in, but there was never a team. Since we were the only girls' team, we would compete against the boys teams. We were all so nervous. We never won, but in one game we were two points away from winning, and we felt really accomplished regardless.

After a year of living in Mexico, we decided to go back to America. So then, that's when we decided to move to Madison a year ago. Here in Madison after school, I take part in a lot of activities. I am part of a robotics team, CyberPatriots, improv club, Scholars of Color, engineering club, and Canstruction. CyberPatriots is a cyber defense team where we compete with other teams across the US, and the competitions are seven hours long. In Canstruction you build things like sculptures out of cans. Scholars of Color is a club for minorities who are taking AP and honors classes, and we try to encourage other minorities to take them as well. A lot of our meetings are study strategies, and we have a presenter once a month who talks about their lives growing up as a minority and how they pushed through regardless, just words of encouragement. So I love to be part of school activities.

One of the biggest things I realized when I first moved to Madison was that there were a lot of opportunities here for me. When I was in Mexico, I limited myself. I'm a completely different person than I was there. It has more to do with personal growth than being in Mexico. "Mexico-me" never would have thought about going into STEM. All my friends either wanted to go into nursing or law or something, so it never came into my mind to go into STEM because I would only hear about it from males. I was always so intimidated by math and science and subjects that are STEM related, but then after I joined my robotics team, I decided I need to go into engineering. My parents are really happy with me about that. Out of all the activities that I do, robotics is the most important to me. I was the only girl for months, and I was forced to defend my credibility and think out loud.

I love creating things—I love the idea that I can keep learning. I will always have questions for the rest of my life that will always be unanswered, so I can always come up with new things. Over the summer I took part in a computer engineering program at the Milwaukee School of Engineering. After that I completely fell in love with circuits, computers, and the idea of computer science, which led me my senior year to sign up for computer science classes and programming classes, which really inspired me to go into it. I got a student achievement award that was given to eight out of five hundred seniors. When I got the award, I had to say some words about my life, and I talked about moving different places and my aspirations.

In the future, I'm planning to major in electrical engineering and minor in computer science here in Madison. I still don't know what school I want to go to. So I guess with what I plan to go into when I go to college, I really want to help inspire other minorities to go into STEM, especially females since it's so intimidating based on gender or ethnicity or race. It's honestly really hard because I felt so scared when I first got into it. There's always going to be someone smarter, that knows more, or is more experienced, but you can do whatever you want. People shouldn't limit themselves based on stereotypes or just because they think they're not socially acceptable. That's why I really want to help inspire women to go into STEM.

VIDEO LINKS

greencardvoices.org/speakers/christine-encarnacion

AFRICA

Tema, Ghana

Nana-Kwesi Konadu

Born: Honolulu, Hawaii   **Raised:** Tema, Ghana
Current City: Madison, WI

> "BEFORE COMING HERE, I DIDN'T THINK THAT THE ACCENT WOULD BE A MAJOR OBSTACLE. PEOPLE FOUND IT VERY HARD TO UNDERSTAND ME IN SCHOOL BECAUSE OF THE DIFFERENCE IN ACCENTS, BECAUSE OF MY SHYNESS, AND BECAUSE I SPOKE QUIETLY."

I was born in Honolulu, Hawaii, in the year 2001. My parents moved to the United States in 1999, so right before I was born. My father came here when he was a teenager. His father, my grandfather, came to the US via the immigration lottery, so he was able to bring my dad and his sisters to the US. My dad from the age of 12 went to high school and college in America. After college he moved back to Ghana, where he met my mom. He joined the US Army, and they sent him to Hawaii, and they both moved to Hawaii, where they had me. After a few years, they moved to Chicago. My two sisters, Nadya and Neena, were born in Chicago. In Chicago they were trying to settle into a new environment where they both had to find new jobs. They needed some help, so they sent me to my grandmother in Ghana. I was around two at the time. I don't remember much from that first time when I was in Ghana.

I did kindergarten in Ghana. After a few years, when my parents had finally attained financial stability, I was brought back to Chicago. After spending a few years in Chicago, because my mother decided to attend dental school, I was sent back to Ghana again. I spent five years in Ghana.

Moving back to Ghana was pretty interesting. Though accompanied by an inevitable shock, I remember my stay in Ghana being characterized by a strong sense of community and support. The town I lived in, Tema, was literally divided into communities. When I look back, I recall often walking out the gates of my house to buy bread. On the way, I remember greeting everyone, and it was really nice to feel like a member of this communal family.

Though the American and Ghanaian school systems were very different, I found little difficulty in adapting to the Ghanaian life. I went to a Lutheran primary school in Ghana. School there was pretty nice. At school I made many friends. We used to play soccer. The school system was very strict. I feel like in Ghana I really developed a strong sense of discipline when it comes to education. The importance of education is heavily emphasized because it is viewed as a pathway to future success.

My sisters and I grew up with our two cousins, Kweku and Ekow. We used to visit them a lot, but at some point they came to live with us in our house in Tema. Sometimes we spent time with our dad, who had moved to Ghana not too long after we did. We would go to a restaurant called Bryan's Place where we would eat sausage kebabs and fried rice. In fact, I really loved the Ghanaian food. My favorite food is jollof rice—it's very, very nice. It's rice that's been stewed in a sauce with tomato, garlic, ginger, pepper, and other ingredients. It really has a nice aroma that fills the kitchen. Ghanaian music is also very nice. I usually listened to hiplife, a genre of music that is like a mix between Ghanaian music and hip hop. Also while in Tema, I really picked up on the Twi language, understanding it and becoming fluent in it. I also gained an appreciation for Ghanaian principles, like being disciplined, showing obedience, serving others before myself, and striving to make the best of the opportunities I have.

In Ghana, I remember just really embracing the life I had. Though I missed my parents dearly, I became accustomed to my new home. The US really became a very distant memory. I just embraced my new home.

Around the time I went to Ghana the second time, my parents were separated, and my mom was in dental school. Because it was very expensive, she decided to do this program with the military, the Air Force, in which they would pay for her education in exchange for three years of her service. And so, she went to dental school. When she finished, she went to Sheppard Air Force Base in Wichita Falls, Texas and worked. My mom got married shortly after completing dental school, although our stepdad continued to live in Madison while my mom was in Texas.

I remember the day that I heard we were moving back to the US. I was very surprised that time had passed by so quickly. I had just recently talked with my mom and didn't expect to finally reunite with her, though I knew the day would eventually arrive. It remained a thing of the distant future. I was going to take my exam around that time for the seventh grade, and just when I felt like I was really making friends and embracing the life to the fullest in Ghana, it was time to move. I really felt conflicting emotions. On one hand, I was so excited to see my mom again and to come to the United States again, but on the other hand, I didn't want to leave my family, my friends, my life, and my culture. I knew that when I came here I would have to give up that identity, and

I wasn't ready to do that.

We were going to fly from Ghana to London, then from London to Dallas, and then drive to my mom in Wichita Falls, Texas. My sisters and I traveled with our grandmother. The journey from Ghana to London was straightforward. I hadn't been on a plane for years, so I was absolutely mesmerized by the opportunity. Once we reached London, though, we were informed that there were snowstorms in the US and that we had to either fly to Philadelphia or wait in London. So we decided to go to Philadelphia. Once we got there, there was so much snow. I was so shocked! After all these years, I knew it was going to be cold because it was in December, but I was not ready for this. I wasn't even wearing the right stuff. During the walk to our hotel, I was surprised by how cold it was.

Though it was really hard, I was so very excited to finally be in the US. After a few days in Philadelphia, we took a plane to Dallas, Texas. Once we got there, I really noticed this stark difference between Philadelphia and Texas. Before, I had always thought everywhere in the US is the same, but I noticed a difference in the weather and in the way people were talking at the airport. We got to Dallas, and then we took another flight to Wichita Falls, Texas, where my mom's Air Force base was. When we got there, I was so shocked. The Air Force base was a whole different world within the town we were in. I was surprised to see the soldiers at the gates, scanning cards. I was surprised to see all the houses that looked the same and all the planes in the sky. It was very nice. The first two weeks in Texas weren't bad. I didn't go to school until February, and I was in seventh grade at the time.

When I come to the US, there were so many changes, so many differences—especially going to school. While in school, I really underwent culture shock. I really realized this was a completely different life from the one I had been used to. I felt like I was getting a lot of stares and people were laughing because of the way I talked and the way I dressed, so it was difficult to make friends. Before coming here, I didn't think that the accent would be a major obstacle. People found it very hard to understand me in school because of the difference in accents, because of my shyness, and because I spoke quietly. I felt like I had to continue to talk and keep explaining myself, and that was hard because it just made me feel like I wasn't communicating, and I felt like that would be a major barrier to embracing the new life. I felt like I had to give up my accent and the way I talked and the way I thought. Aside from that, I dressed very differently from others, so that also garnered attention. The accent and the way I dressed were things that I felt like I had to change, but aside from that it was very difficult to make friends as well. Coming from Ghana I thought I could just go up to people and say, "Oh hi, my name is Nana," but I was so shy. I was so scared of rejection, so I really kept to myself during that time. But after a few months, I started to come out of my shell and try to initiate more conversations. I slowly stopped trying to change my accent and just accepted who I was. I realized that it didn't matter how I talked and that it didn't matter if people didn't understand me. I knew that with time I would eventually pick up on the American accent and make some friends. After a while I did pick up on the new accent and made many more friends as I opened up. Through that experience I learned to embrace who I was, and I continue to strive to embrace the new life.

After the three years of her contract with the Air Force were complete, in the year of 2016, my mother decided to move us to Madison where our stepdad lives. It was very, very different. Madison was this dynamic place. It was the closest place that I felt came to the view of the US as a place with opportunity. This place had a downtown area and an exciting vibe.

I had just started high school when we moved, I completed ninth grade in Texas. I started tenth grade in Madison. The school systems were very similar, and the courses were very similar. I found that there were more academic opportunities in my Madison school. By that time I had really embraced the American school system, so this move was a very easy transition.

It was in my new school that I came to discover that I have a deep passion for science. The science we did back in Ghana was more focused on agricultural aspects, like growing plants and maintaining farms. Coming to America and learning about biology and chemistry, I really figured out that this is what I really love to do. The fact that these subjects could be used to explain various process that contribute to human life really intrigues me. Today I continue to pursue this passion for science, participating in a variety of activities like Science Bowl, Science Olympiad, and tutoring my peers in science.

A few summers ago, I got the opportunity to do research at the Wisconsin Institute for Medical Research at UW-Madison. I'm involved in a lot of volunteering too. I'm the vice president of Key Club, which is like the Kiwanis Club, and I love to volunteer at the food pantry over the weekends and volunteer at elementary school fairs and such. Aside from that I'm very invested in school. I try to take the hardest classes so I can challenge myself continually and maintain the emphasis on education that I picked up when I was in Ghana.

In the future, I want to go into oncology and become an oncologist so that one day I can return to Ghana and other third world countries and help address the issue of childhood cancer. While in Ghana, I realized that many people are suffering from more treatable cancer conditions due to inadequate medical care, lack of resources, and the fact that there are very few trained oncologists in Ghana. I hope to perhaps one day return with a team of fellow researchers to investigate potential herbal remedies. Aside from that, I'd also love to travel the world. I feel like there are so many places to go and many perspectives I can pick up. As for living, I'll either live in a big city somewhere in the US or move back to Ghana. But I'm sure I'll be coming here very often if I move to Ghana.

Right now my dad lives in Belgium, Brussels, so during the summer and some winter breaks, my sisters and I get the opportunity to go to Brussels. This past summer we got to spend two months there, and this really provided me with an appreciation for European culture. And so I feel like this has helped me to refine my perspective. I continue to embrace my Ghanaian culture. At home I continue to speak the Twi language with my parents, continue to eat the food, continue to call my relatives every week. My family and I are members of the Ghana Association of Madison, a group that organizes celebrations for Ghanaian holidays, such as Ghanaian Independence Day, as well as provides support to Ghanaian-Americans and immigrants in Madison. I take from the American perspective . . . I take from the newly-attained European perspective . . . and I continue to maintain my Ghanaian perspective.

VIDEO LINKS

greencardvoices.org/speakers/nana-kwesi-konadu

ASIA

Baghdad, Iraq

Ruqayah Alkhrsa

From: Baghdad, Iraq
Current City: Madison, WI

"MY SCHOOL EXPERIENCE WAS AWESOME. AND I THINK WE CONCENTRATED A LOT ON SCHOOL TO TAKE OUR MINDS OFF OF WHAT WAS GOING ON AROUND US. MY TEACHERS WERE EXCELLENT, AND MY CLASSMATES WERE MY DEAREST FRIENDS."

My life in Baghdad was really good. I had friends and family there. It was really comfortable. But Iraq wasn't safe at all because of the war. Sometimes, I can still hear bombs exploding at 4:00 a.m. I was born in 2000, and the war started when I turned three years old, so I don't really know how it was before. I know that we moved three times during the war, which was during my childhood. We first lived in Baghdad, which was the most safe place back then. But it quickly became unsafe, so we moved to where my grandparents lived. We thought it would be safer, but it turned out it wasn't because it got worse and worse after a few months. Heavy bombing started within a month of our move, so we moved again to another area we thought was safer. But that didn't last long, and we realized that no place was safe in the entire city! So, we moved again to another area we thought it would be safer, but it wasn't. We left everything behind because our lives were in danger. We spent like four or five months in the new location. Finally we decided to go back to our original house and we stayed there until 2006. We moved again to another house because of safety basically. This new area was better because my aunt's house was in that area, too, so we were closer and could go visit each other.

We still were able to go to school despite all the fighting and bombing around us. I remember one day in my elementary school when we had to leave quickly because there was a real bomb placed in the school. Fortunately, it was defused before it exploded, and that time no one was injured. I went to school until ninth grade in Iraq. I spent a lot of my life there. My school experience in Iraq was awesome. The teachers were really good. My friends were the best. I could say they were my dear good friends. I miss them. Some of them are still there and happily living. Good thing is I haven't lost any of my best friends through the war. I miss them a lot, but we are still in touch.

I remember it was a warm day during September 2016, when we were still on summer vacation from school, we had a family meeting. My dad said, "We'll move to the U.S." The first thing that came to my mind: "Oh my god, I'm gonna leave my friends." I told them that I am moving to the U.S., and they were like, "Oh my god, you are leaving. Like really leaving." Everything was like a little bit happy, but it was mostly sad. My mom wasn't really happy because she didn't want to move, but my dad wanted to make a new life. So we decided—or he decided and then told us— and tried to make us go with him. He succeeded. Just two months earlier, my brother was almost killed when he and his friends were on the street just talking. I guess my parents couldn't risk the danger anymore. My dad worked with the U.S. troops from 2008 to 2012, and all of the people who worked with the Americans were given a special visa to move because of fears for their safety. We were one of the last people of the group to leave.

Some people were glad for us, but many family and friends were sad to see us go. My mom was sad, but my dad said that we needed to be safe and to make a new life. We went from house to house saying goodbye to our relatives. Arab families love to have meals together, and so our family and friends wanted to invite us to have a gathering for a last time before we left. We left Baghdad on my brother's birthday, October 9, 2016. So my aunt made a birthday party for him and gathered everybody. I stayed up the whole night with my cousin just talking and then crying a lot in the end. I remember crying with my grandmother because she was so sad we were leaving. My mom was crying too—it was a sad night. My parents already packed our things and did all the work the week before, so we didn't have anything in the house. We just went to our relatives to say goodbye on the very last day.

We flew from Iraq to Jordan. We stayed in Jordan the whole night. Then we flew from Jordan to Chicago O'Hare airport and it took thirteen hours. I watched a movie and slept a little. It was a really long flight. I had been on an airplane before but just for an hour, so this flight seemed so long. When we came to Madison the very first people we met here was my father's friend and the caseworker to help us settle in Madison. It was really late at night. It was probably 12:00 or 1:00 a.m., so I didn't see anything because it was really dark, and I was so sleepy because we had such a long journey from Jordan to here. They took us to a hotel the first night, and we stayed there. They came in the morning to take us to our new house, which they'd set up for us, so we didn't really have anything to do.

The weather was so different. It was during October, and it was fall here, but it was cold for me because it was still kind of summer back in Iraq. The weather was so different, but now I don't even notice the seasons, and I'm happy to say the changes of seasons feels normal to me. In Baghdad we just had two seasons, and it never got very cold. Winter there is kind of like fall here.

The very few first days I mostly stayed in the house, unpacking my luggage because we just came here, so we had to organize our closet. We didn't really go out that much because no one knew the directions. We could call the caseworkers, but we didn't ask them to take us out because they had work. We couldn't just say, "Come here and leave your work." So we just stayed indoors until we got familiar with the area. Our first outing was when my dad's friend took us shopping at Target.

When we got here, we were asking about school. I remember me and my sister we were so excited to go to school. I was in tenth grade I was so excited to start school. But when I did start school I didn't like it. It was so different from my old school that I didn't really like it here. I started school in Madison on my sixteenth birthday, and it didn't feel much like a celebration at all. My high school became familiar though. Now it's my new school, and I am used to it.

The main difference was language. It was a whole different language, different alphabet, and writing from left to right and not right to left. In Iraq we studied English, but when I came here, it was like "what, this is not the English I studied." I had to learn everything from the start. At school, people were so close with each other—I couldn't really fit the very first year. I don't have that outgoing personality, so that was really hard, too. It was shocking because I couldn't fit in with the people. Now I've been here for two years—this is my third year, and I'm a senior. I just started a new school year two months ago. My life right now is going easier than when I started here. Now I have friends, so I usually hang out with them or talk to them during and after school. On the weekends, I just relax because school has been really stressing me out. I live with my parents (my mom and dad), my two older brothers, and my younger sister.

Last year I took chemistry, It was the most fun class I ever took in my whole life. Not only here in the U.S. but anywhere. It wasn't only a subject,: it was a whole different experience. I liked that a lot. I liked math too, but it's super hard here. Other school subjects are just fine. The most memorable one though was chemistry. I really still remember everything from last year.

I am a senior now, and I'm thinking about what major should I choose next year in college. I am planning to continue studying in college, and I am choosing biochemistry for my major. Before choosing biochemistry, I was thinking of being a neurologist in the future, but I don't want to be a neurologist anymore. I changed my mind and have chosen biochemistry because ever since I entered high school, the classes I enjoyed the most were biology and chemistry. Biology was an interesting course, especially the labs. The whole course was full of new knowledge, and I loved that I kept learning so much the entire year. And obviously I liked chemistry. My major really changed this year, so I don't really know what I will be in the future. If you asked me last year, I would say a neurologist and now I say: "Let's see what the future will bring."

VIDEO LINKS

greencardvoices.org/speakers/ruqayah-alkhrsa

Yanci Almonte Vargas

From: Santiago de los Caballeros, Dominican Republic
Current City: Madison, WI

"I KNOW IT'S REALLY HARD RIGHT NOW BUT KEEP GOING. NEVER LET THE DARKNESS TURN OFF YOUR LIGHT."

My name is Yanci Almonte, and I'm from the Dominican Republic, a small island in the Caribbean ocean. While I lived there, life was a struggle because my mom was a single mother, and she didn't have many resources. The economic situation there is not the best—the politics and the people in charge are really corrupt. It was okay, but there was just this factor always there, the economic situation. And, my father was never in the picture . . . so yeah.

Most of my life I went to school in Dominican Republic. I went through sixth grade, and then I did seventh grade in Pennsylvania. Then I went back and did eighth grade in Dominican Republic. I went back to Pennsylvania and did ninth grade, and from then on I've done the other years in Madison. Going to school in the DR was challenging because I used to get bullied a lot for being overweight and shy. I just helped my mom work in her business. She's a veterinarian. She works with animals, and she basically sells the food for the animals and treatment and all these kinds of things. So, I would help her in her small business.

Because my mom is a veterinarian, I grew up to like animals, especially dogs. I've had three dogs, but right now I don't have one because of the time it takes. My last dog was a chihuahua, and her name was Gira. I had three years with her, but then she got stolen the first year after I came to the US. Because my mom was working, she had to leave the dog with a neighbor, and the neighbor lost sight of the dog.

When I was twelve years old, I was notified by my dad that I was going to live in America because my dad's sister applied for the whole family to come legally to America. Even though my dad was not there my whole life, he contacted my mom in the process of the application and asked her if she would like for me to be included in the process. The immigration process took twelve

35

years. He was like, "This is something good for Yanci. Even though I have not done a lot for him in the past, this is something that will benefit him."

When I left home, it was very exciting but also very scary because it was a new life. It was a dream coming true because, you know, you are like . . . a kid, then you are like, "Oh my God, the USA." I've always dreamt of coming to the US. And it was not that hard at the moment.

I was coming to the US with my dad's wife, her dog, my aunt from my dad's side, and her family. My mom dropped me at the airport, and then we met with them. Then my mom said, "Bye," and we took off in the airplane. When we got to the US, we arrived at New York City, and then my uncle took us to Philadelphia, Pennsylvania. When I got there, I started living with my dad and getting to know his family.

Getting to know my dad's family was kind of weird because I was born outside of his marriage, so he didn't raise me. But because I was born outside of his marriage, I was kind of the unlawful kid. It's the wrong term, but that's how I felt. So, it was kind of like they would accept me as family, but I'm not entirely family because you can see that they treat you different and all these things. And it was just like, I'm out of place, and my mom told me like, "You're going to have to behave good and make a good impression because his family doesn't accept you but mostly because his wife doesn't."

When I first got to America, the school was really different because of the language, the population of the school, and the structure of the system of the school. It was hard to transition from speaking Spanish every day and knowing what to say to not knowing what you're trying to say in a different language. The school was mainly dominated by African American students. There weren't many people I could speak Spanish with. It was not a really diverse school. It was like a private school. You had to wear uniforms, and even though I had to wear them in my native country, it was more rigorous in Pennsylvania. I didn't have that many friends, and it was just like kind of a different structure. I used to get out of school at 12:00 p.m. in the Dominican Republic, but now I was getting out at 4:00 p.m.

As time passed, I realized the cold truth—I was not able to see my mom and my family from my mom's side. I was not able to help my mom anymore. And I had to make new friends and new family because I had never lived with my dad and his family. I was shy, so it did not help at all.

When I got to America, it was summer, but it was already kind of cold because it's Pennsylvania. It's always kind of like that chill air, so it's never like fully summer. You had to wear like long pants. I like the warm weather more because you wear shorts, and all these things. Also, the life here is like you have to be inside your house or the church or to your family's. If you're going to do something, you do it quick, but then you get into your house, and you spend most of your time enclosed in your house. And it was so weird because I can just walk outside in my native country, go to the neighbors, and be like, "Hey, how are you," and we like trade food and all these things. And it's like different here, you have to be enclosed just in your house. It was weird, and you kind of get depressed because you're like, "What am I supposed to do here? I don't have homework. I don't have anything to do." There's just like TV or sleeping or studying, and there's not much sun, and it's cold.

So, I moved from Pennsylvania like three years ago. Basically I spent the year there with my dad, my first year in the US. But then things didn't work out because his family, they didn't like me, especially his wife, so I went back to the Dominican Republic. I stayed there for a year. Then I came back to Pennsylvania again for another year to live with a guardian, but things didn't work out either with that woman. Then, during the summer of that year, 2016, I went back to the Dominican Republic and spent the summer there. And my mom was like, "Do you want to go back to the US, even though you've had these bad experiences?" And I was like, "I don't." But she contacted this friend who I live with now, and she was like, "You can try it, but if you don't like it then you can go back after a month." And I was like, "Okay."

So, I came to Madison, and I spent a month. I was like, "Everything's okay, Mami, so I think I'll stay." And basically from then on it's been great. I'm more open . . . I'm more extroverted . . . I've gotten out of my bubble. Now I'm not so shy. The family where I live now is basically like my family here because, even if we're not blood related, they treat me like one—even if there's a money issue, like my mom still has to pay for me to live here. She's doing it because she wants me to get a better education and have success. And I know the language, which helps.

My normal day would be like waking up, breakfast, and then every day I have a club. Today at lunch I have Green Club. I'm also part of AVID and Scholars of Color. I wanted to go into that because it's a club for people of color that are not Caucasian. We meet people of color that take AP courses, and they bring speakers of color to talk about their lives and their success in the US. I'm part of a lot of clubs, so like every day at lunch I have a club. I take three AP classes. During the weekends I mostly have family gatherings, like after church we go to someone's house from the family, and we have lunch or sometimes we go shopping. For Thanksgiving, that just passed, we did a whole dinner and danced after and just met and talked. And I also have three Latinx friends that I hang out with.

In the future I want to go to college and study something that helps me help people. I don't know yet, but I'm thinking of becoming a doctor. I don't know . . . I just want to do something to help people. Even if it's not helping immigrants directly but just helping people overall because I didn't get that much help when I first came here, and I wish I had. I know I struggled when I first came here, and I still struggle. But now I've got it here in Madison. There are amazing people here, and I just want to give back to this country that has been amazing to me and make it better because there are many things that the US can improve on and that my country can improve on. If I can be part of that, then I'm going to be part of it. Because I don't know if I'm going to study and then end up in my country, I may study something that helps me here, but I can also help people there—like being a doctor.

I just want to tell the people, keep going—especially immigrants. I know it's really hard right now but keep going. Never let the darkness turn off your light. Be you. And your accent—don't change it, keep it. Be you, and just shine with your light. Don't let people put you down. Even if it's another language, you can learn it. It may take time, but you can do it. Get out of your comfort zone because if I hadn't done that here in Madison, I wouldn't be the person that I am right now. I've met amazing people that have taught me and have changed me in a lot of different ways that I may not have done if I hadn't opened up to new things. Be open-minded and just strive for higher things. The sky's the limit, like they say.

VIDEO LINKS

greencardvoices.org/speakers/yanci-almonte-vargas

ASIA

Aleppo, Syria

Selma Fustok

Born: Madison, WI   **Raised:** Aleppo, Syria
Current City: Madison, WI

> "WRITING OUT MY ANSWERS FOR THIS PROJECT MADE ME REFLECT ON WHAT I'VE BEEN THROUGH...I REALIZED MY FAMILY DID SO MUCH FOR ME TO BE HERE."

I was born in Madison, Wisconsin, and my parents were born in Syria. My dad went to college here, and my brother, who is two years older than me, was born here as well and is now attending UW Madison.

The United States felt like home . . . but not really. I knew I was Syrian and that my parent's family and my family were back home. We didn't know Arabic that well, but we knew enough words to simply say "hi" to our grandparents back home. It felt like we were always planning on moving there.

I was in kindergarten the year we left. I remember memories of my friends playing around. My mom was a teacher, and we went to the same school; I remember being with her and the rides back home. We used to always get Subway and go on walks to the parks and lakes.

I was confused because I was leaving all my friends, and I was really young. When we moved to Aleppo, Syria, I knew some Arabic, but I was really shy. All of my cousins were trying to talk to me, but I didn't know what they were saying. Overtime I caught on with the language. I don't even remember it cause of how fast it happened. It was really nice being around family and just growing up there.

The culture was very different, but I did not mind it because I got to learn about my people. I learned more about language and religion and the culture of Syria, the Middle East in general, and the systems of school and family by living there.

I went to an Islamic private school where many of my teachers wanted me specifically to wear the hijab. Some of the other girls wore it but others didn't. Although other girls didn't wear it, the teachers didn't pressure them as much as they pressured me. I really wanted to wear it. My parents understood that I wanted to wear it because of the school's pressure and not of my own will,

41

which was why they didn't let me wear it when I asked to.

Usually a girl's supposed to start wearing it after puberty, but I hadn't hit that yet. I hit puberty, and they gave me time to think about it because they wanted me to choose with intention, knowing that it's not just a game. A lot of people decide not to wear it, which is understandable, but I wanted to put it on. I knew from the people around me what it was and the rules about it but not really the reason behind wearing it, but I still wore it with my own intention.

If you are American in Syria, some people are always like, "Oh, can you say something in English?" I didn't like that because I just wanted to be treated the same. Some people like being "the American girl," but I didn't like it at all. In America it is the same, but it's more of a big deal. Some people are interested and have a lot of questions, like "What's your religion?" or "Can you say something in Arabic?" I never really liked all that attention.

We lived there for five years. The last year I was in Syria, the war was starting, but no one knew that it was going to be a big thing. It was small events that were recurring. I remember some things, like when we would hear gunshots, but we lived in an area where there were lots of empty lands. We weren't close to the city and that was the area that was attacked in the beginning. Things would happen that we would hear of around us, so the first thing we did was pack a little bit and take the things we needed and went to the city where my grandma lived. We stayed there for about a month hoping that things would get better around our house, but unfortunately things got worse, and it was becoming less safe in the city area. We realized that it was time to leave.

My parents felt concerned in case we had to come back to the United States because my passport had been expired. The only way we could get it renewed was if we went to Beirut in Lebanon, so we went. We hoped we would stay there a few weeks and then come back, as we kept thinking it'd get better. We didn't think it was a permanent thing.

We went to Beirut and got the passport renewed. I remember my parents talking; they said we were about to get tickets to go back to the States. Things were not looking good back home, so we couldn't go back. My parents are both teachers, so they both found jobs and schools for us, which was why we decided to stay a little bit longer. I was still in middle school and so was my brother. The plan had always been to return to the United States for college because schools are much better here, but we didn't really think about it much.

We stayed in Beirut for three years, and during these three years it was weird. Moving between two Middle Eastern countries, you wouldn't think it would be that different, but it really was because Lebanese people are not the best with Syrians. Specifically, it was really hard to rent houses and find jobs because they mistreated us. Rent was higher, and it was harder for Syrians to get jobs. There were a lot of homeless Syrian people in Lebanon. A lot of Syrians moved to Lebanon because it was the closest, and the Lebanese didn't like that. I went from "American girl" to "Syrian girl." It wasn't the best stage in my life because it was really hard to blend in with the other school kids. When my brother was getting close to college, we thought we should probably head back to the United States, so we decided to come back here.

My brother is very different from me because he grew up in the United States. He had spent more time here, so for him the United States was more "home," but for me it was Syria because that's where I spent most of my childhood. When we were informed that we were going back to the States, he was really excited about it. I was excited, but more nervous because my English had worn off and I had to relearn it. We learned French instead of English, that's the second language in Lebanon, so I was nervous about re-adjusting my language. I remembered my American friends as kids, but I had been gone for eight years. You can't expect to come back and just reconnect. I was a little bit worried; I knew some friends, but I couldn't expect things to be the way things were. I knew some people here.

Coming back, I had to change my mental image of the United States—it would not be like how I left it. I came back two days before school started, and I didn't have time to adapt to the change of just moving. Now I also had to adapt to the change of schools. We came back to Madison, and some of my friends didn't remember me, which was expected, but we remember each other now. I had to make new friends which I wasn't excited about. In America it's different—at schools back in Syria you're the one that stays in the class and the teacher moves. It's like one class, and you are with these people for a whole year. You get really close to them. Here, I would get close to someone in one period, but it was just for that period, not a friendship. Classes-wise and friendship-wise it was really weird. I had the memory of the United States and Madison with the mentality of a kindergartener, and I came back with the mentality of a high schooler. I know both places aren't the best, but back home wasn't bad as it could get: people would fist fight, but I didn't know about drugs until I came here. It is a very different culture.

Back there the majority of the people are Muslims, so it wasn't like I had to learn about my religion. When I came back to the United States, I had to learn because I had to explain it to other people. Being there, you grow up through the culture and your religion. You don't have to learn about it, and nobody asks you why you wear your scarf or why you do these things. You never explain it. So at fourteen, I had to go back and learn to do the things I should've known.

I was a little bit worried about my scarf, but I personally haven't had any problems with it in my four years of high school. Maybe I'm the only one like that. Many people think it is weird, but I just don't care. I don't think something someone's going to tell me or do to me is going to affect the way I think or believe about myself and my religion. I know a lot of girls that have gone through stuff with it, but I haven't. I have people that sometimes ask me about why I wear it. I never really had to explain back home, so the first time I was asked was my first answering. It's part of my religion. You don't really have to explain it to the people in your community; it's for the people outside. If someone's asking you, it's really embarrassing if you don't know—cause if you don't know, why are you wearing it?

Coming here, the Muslim community is very different. Back there everyone is Muslim, so there's not really one community. Here there is one, but the celebrations are different. In Syria and Lebanon celebrations are more of a known event. Everyone celebrates it there, so everyone knows about it. Here it's just you.

When I came here, the next day was Eid, so I was really excited about it, but it was not the same. I was just like, "Oh, I guess this is how it is." It doesn't feel like a "celebration" celebration. It's more like just buying new clothes. This is part of it, but back there everyone's celebrating, so it's a really different feeling.

Writing out my answers for this project made me reflect on what I've been through. I never really thought of it out loud, and growing up with it, you think about yourself like "I went through all this," but when I was writing about it and thinking about it out loud, I realized my family did so much for me to be here. Now that I'm more mature, I remember things that happened, like I was going through school problems, but then my parents were going through other problems as well. You don't realize that, and you don't value the fact that your parents really want the best for you and your family. I can't imagine having my own kids and having to move from country to country looking for the best living you can give them.

Right now, my dad's side (my first cousins and uncles) were able to flee to Germany. My grandparents both had visas to come to the United States, so they are usually staying with my family, my uncle's family in California, or even sometimes in Germany. On my mom's side, some of her siblings were able to go to New York, but some of them are still in Syria. My grandma and my aunt are still back in Syria.

My mom visited last summer and went to see her. It's never going to be completely safe, but it has gotten to the point where people just have to live with it. You have to expect and accept the fact that something could happen to you. You can't just sit at home—you have to work. People still have jobs. Everything's really messed up there, but most of my mom's side are back home. We keep checking in on them, but you never know what could happen. You could talk to them and they're fine and then find out in the news that something happened and you're like, "I was just talking to them".

I am a senior right now and I'm looking forward to graduating. I'm hoping to go either to UW-Madison or community college because I'm not sure what I want to major in. I'm interested in different things, so I'm not sure at the moment. I work at a tutoring center outside of school, and I also tutor Arabic one-on-one. I do an astrophysics internship to see if I'm interested in that field. At the moment I'm just looking forward to graduating and figuring out what I want to do. I'm hoping after college, after getting my degree, to work a little bit, and then I really want to travel the world and look at and explore different people, cultures, and religions. I hope one day I get to go back and visit Syria.

VIDEO LINKS

greencardvoices.org/speakers/selma-fustok

NORTH AMERICA

Esteli,
Nicaragua

Harield Acuna

Born: Madison, WI   **Raised:** Esteli, Nicaragua
Current City: Madison, WI

> "I ALWAYS JUST PRESENT MYSELF AS WHO I AM. I DON'T WANT TO KEEP MYSELF CHAINED TO ANY PARTICULAR IDENTITY. IF SOMEONE EVER ASKED ME, I USUALLY JUST TELL THEM, 'I'M MIXED.' BUT THEN AGAIN, THEY ALWAYS ASK, 'MIXED WITH WHAT?'"

My family history is pretty convoluted. The furthest I know, it goes back to the Garifuna people that originated in West Nigeria, I believe. They were one of the first Africans to be enslaved and brought to the Americas. However, they were shipwrecked or they escaped, and landed in South America. They managed to live with the natives in the area. From there, a lot of them migrated to mainland Central America, and that's where my family originally comes from. Belize is where my great grandmother was born. She later moved to Nicaragua where she had my grandmother. I also have my grandfather's story, which is actually a bit simpler. He was orphaned at a young age and later trained with American Marines during the 1930s when Nicaragua was occupied by the United States. His daughter, my mom, was raised during the Nicaraguan revolution.

I was born here in Madison, Wisconsin. But when I was just a baby, couple months old, we went to Nicaragua. I do have very vivid memories of what I experienced as a young child. My mom describes moving back to Nicaragua as probably the most irresponsible thing she's ever done. She tells me that it was done to, I guess, show me humility and to connect me to my roots, and to remind me that even though I was born in the US, I will not get spoiled.

I remember having a really happy childhood in Nicaragua. I had a lot of friends growing up, and we always played outside. Right now there's again a political crisis in Nicaragua. I lived there with my mom and usually with other family members that were close friends. I did go to school, including preschool starting at age two. I had a lot of friends, and I do remember hanging out a lot with one of my cousins. His name was David, and I had a best friend who was called Stephen. I did go to the usual Nicaraguan school for first grade. From what I remember, it was a terrible experience because I didn't like the fact that we had to wear a uniform all day. I think I got into a lot of fights when I was little. But I did end up graduating, even with the teachers still hating me. I never thought of myself as too smart, even though, I guess, my educational background would say so.

The main reason why I moved back to the US was that I had a couple cousins who received death threats. They thought of coming here through political asylum. My mom didn't want me to grow up in an environment that would promote negative behavior. I was happy about the move. I saw it more as like a trip than anything life-changing. I honestly thought as myself as an American. I went to the US Embassy once, and I even remember at four years old that I actually kissed the ground like they do in the movies.

At first we moved to Milwaukee and lived there with my mom's boyfriend for a little bit. Then we decided to move back to Madison. It's here that I started second grade. I lived with one of my aunts and her two sons. Honestly, I didn't see it as too different from Nicaragua other than the buildings were bigger. I remember going to this Turkish supermarket, and the owner realized that I was new to the neighborhood and actually gave me free candy.

When I started school in Madison, I noticed a difference: people tended to be very social here compared to Nicaragua. There you're usually encouraged to just shut up and listen.

Looking at my test scores in the second grade, I didn't do too well. But that was probably because I didn't know English. But I did eventually learn it about a year in, and I actually graduated from ESL after just a year in the program. In terms of friends, I made a lot. I still have some friends from second grade that I still hang out with to this day. I remember we played superhero and airplane a lot of times during recess.

Three days of the week after school I go to work, and if I'm not working, I do try to study. I work at Gino's Italian Deli. I make the sandwiches, wash the dishes, and look over the kitchen. I like it there. It's nice a place to work at, even though it might be a bit labor intensive. I started working there because one of my aunts also used to work there and recommended the place to me as a nice first job.

I'm usually too busy to do a lot of after-school activities. I used to be in Latinos Unidos, and I did enjoy my experience there. I hope if I get some more free time that I could go back and participate a bit more.

I would say the biggest thing I gave up coming to the USA was spending time with my dad. The only thing I can do now is call him over the phone.

Yeah. He's very vocal whenever we talk and always asks me, "You're going to come back, right?" And I tell him, "Maybe when I'm older, I'll go back and visit you guys."

I hope to be a software engineer and have that as a career goal. That's really the main thing that I'm focusing on. I teach myself coding in whatever spare time I've got. It started when I was around fourteen. I knew I wanted to get into something with engineering, then it transitioned into wanting to work with technology and computers. I just got more specific as the time went on. When I was in middle school, I decided to become a software engineer once I realized I had some experience with code. I did coding for a bit, and I wanted to see if I could translate those skills into a career. Do I want to make anything in particular? I don't really have an idea.

In terms of identity, it's kind of weird because many people aren't used to having mixed racial makeup be a big part of their identity. Since I'm part White, part Black, and part Native American, it's very important to me. I guess that's still considered a foreign concept to a lot of people here in the United States, especially to other Latinos, and I have friends who see me as Black. I have friends who think I'm White, and none of them would ever associate me with any type of Latino culture. I'm like a weird mix of identities in a way.

I always try to make race not that big of an issue. I always just present myself as who I am. I don't want to keep myself chained to any particular identity. If someone ever asked me, I usually just tell them, "I'm mixed." But then again, they always ask, "Mixed with what?" And that's when I start getting into the details, and I guess my main worry would be that me saying something about it, about my ethnicity, would change the way they view me.

VIDEO LINKS

greencardvoices.org/speakers/harield-acuna

ASIA

Arunachal
Pradesh, India

Dickshya Gurung

Born: Arunachal Pradesh, India **Raised:** Beldangi, Nepal
Current City: Madison, WI

"THERE WERE A LOT OF PEOPLE WHO TOLD ME, 'YOU ARE SO BIG AND YOU'RE ONLY IN GRADE ONE? YOU CAN'T STUDY.' THEY LAUGHED AT ME AND MADE FUN OF ME. BUT ONE GOOD THING WAS THAT THERE WERE A LOT OF PEOPLE, INCLUDING MY BROTHER AND MY FAMILY, WHO ENCOURAGED ME."

Life was difficult when I was a child. I grew up mostly in India, and there I lived with my mother and stepdad, and it was really difficult for me because they didn't love me. What I wanted most was for them to love me, and I was never sure how to make that happen.

I had to take care of my two stepsisters. I didn't go to school anymore after I was ten years old. That part of my life was really difficult for many reasons. My mom and my stepdad are alcoholics. I was physically and mentally abused. My stepdad always told me, "I am the child without a father," and it made me really sad. Sometimes I would cry, and I thought, "I don't have anyone; nobody loves me." I even tried to kill myself. I also worked really hard because I had to take care of my two sisters. When my mom first got married to my stepdad, he loved me, and he took care of me. Then when my mom had his baby, he didn't care about me anymore. I always ran away from him; I was scared of him. Whenever I didn't do some work or if he thought I didn't care for my stepsisters, he slapped me. I always dreamed about knowing my real father and brother, but at the time I thought they were dead.

My mom told me, "You have no brother, you have no sister, you don't have anyone except us." I really believed her and I always cried. My friends and neighbors in India would always tell me, "If there is any possibility in your future, if your father comes to take you, please go with him." I didn't believe them and I thought, "That's not going to be possible because I don't have a father." That's what my mom told me, and I believed her.

When I was ten years old, I found out that I have a father. On the day my father came to meet me, I was really surprised. My father told me, "I'm going to take you. I'm going to take you away from this problem." At first I didn't believe him because I believed my mom when she told me, "You don't have a father." So now, how could I believe him? I didn't believe him at first. But he talked to me two or three times, and I started believing him. After that, I told my mom, "I want to go with my dad. I don't want to live with you guys anymore because you don't care about me, and I'm not going to school. You guys are not sending me to school, and I don't have an education." My mom said, "No, you can't go," and my stepdad told me, "You can't go because we are the ones who take care of you." I knew they took care me since childhood, but there were a lot of things they needed to give me, like a good education and a good life. But they didn't give me that, so I decided to go with my dad. I wanted to go with my dad if he wanted to give me a good life, so in 2010, I decided to move to Nepal with my dad.

I was ten years old when I moved to Nepal with my dad. The first time I saw my stepmom she was sitting outside and my dad told me, "She is your mom from now on," and I was nervous like, "Oh my gosh. How will I call her mom when she's not my mom?" I got a new sister too. My dad told me, "You have to call her sister, and you have to think about her like she's your sister starting today." I went into the home and I called my new mom, "Ama," the Nepali word for mom. It was difficult because she's not my mom, but I called them "Ama," "Didi" or "sister," so they would love me. I was so surprised I got a good sister.

In Nepal I started going to school. I started grade one when I was ten years old. In a refugee camp, kids in grade one are probably seven or eight years old. I was 10 years old—I was really big, and I went to school for the first time with my brother. There were a lot of people who told me, "You are so big and you're only in grade one? You can't study." They laughed at me and made fun of me. But one good thing was that there were a lot of people, including my brother and my family, who encouraged me. They told me, "Don't care about what other people think. You just study; we are with you." I thought, 'Wow, they are with me.' After a difficult start, I started thinking, "Well, I'm not gonna care about other people. I'm here. I'm going to school because I want a good education, I want to learn; I want to do something in my life."

After all, an education is not going to tell you, "You're big, or you're small." It's only people who do that. People are the ones who make fun of others. Even my cousins told me, "You are big, but we are in grade five, and you're still in grade two." But soon I started to like learning, and I studied really hard, and then I beat them! They failed class and stayed in grade six! I beat them, and then I studied with them. I studied there for six years, and then we started the process to come to the United States with my parents, my brother, and my grandmother.

It was difficult to come to the US. First, we didn't have any of my documents from India. But with time, my dad collected all the important documents for us, and then we started to apply to come to the US. After four years they finally accepted us. When they accepted the application, I was really surprised, and I was really happy inside of my heart. But I was a little bit sad because, at the same time, I had to leave my school friends and some of my family. But I was really happy that me and my family were allowed to move to the US. I learned a bit of English in Nepal, and my brother can speak English, but we had a lot of problems on our journey. When we left for the airport and our trip, it was difficult just to find the bathroom and where to go eat. Our trip took a whole day, and I didn't like the food on the airline.

But after a long trip, we came to Madison. It was winter and I remember it was a really cold day like I never felt before! When we came to Madison and I saw so much snow, I was so surprised. It was November 16, 2016, and our new life was beginning in the snow and cold.

When we arrived, it was night, and my sister and brother-in-law came to take us to their home because we didn't have a home yet as new people in the US. I'm really thankful my sister and her husband were already settled here and could help us when we came here.

At first everything was very shocking. When I entered their home, oh my gosh, I remember such weird smells, and to me it smelled so bad. I was getting nervous, and I started saying, "Oh my, I want to go back to Nepal, I want to go back." At first I stayed home for three months, but I started to worry about learning English.

When I finally went out, I remember shopping with my brother-in-law. He took me and my sister out to stores like Burlington, Walmart, and Woodman's, and I was surprised there were so many people and that they were different from us and that everyone was speaking English. Sometimes people would say, "Hi," and I just said, "Hmm," and then, "Um." At first when I went to the store, my brother-in-law helped me lot, speaking in English whenever I needed him.

We also had two refugee caseworkers who helped us a lot. I am really thankful for them. They helped me register for school. At school one teacher asked me some questions and it was really difficult to answer, but I started high school classes after I took a test and filled out some paperwork. My first challenge was learning English.

At first when I went to school, I didn't know where the bus stopped, and I was very confused and nervous. When I went to the class, there were a lot of people speaking Spanish and English, and I was just quiet at first, but I am really thankful to my teachers and family and all the people who supported me. In my free time, I love to read and sing. I learned to sing more because I had to lead with my church family or my choir team, so I love to sing. I love Christian songs because I'm Christian. I met a lot of nice people through the church. I also do community service by leading a youth group there.

Now I have a part time job at a grocery store. When I went to the interview, I was worried about my language, but the manager was good. She helped me out. I work at the courtesy desk right now, and it's really good. "Courtesy" means just helping the customer with whatever they need help with and I like it. At first, I learned a lot of English working in the bakery because it was difficult for me to speak English when helping a customer. One of the most difficult jobs is when we take phone orders because there are so many questions and answers we have to get right.

My future plan is to study hard. Next year I plan to graduate from high school and start college. I will keep trying to improve my English through hard work and study. First, I will learn to be a Certified Nursing Assistant (CNA). That will teach me about medicine and help me to earn a living while I continue to study. I will work hard at everything so I can do something for my family. In the future I want to become a registered nurse (RN) because I love to help old people. I really love to help whoever needs my help, and I think a career in healthcare will be the best way to reach my dream.

VIDEO LINKS

greencardvoices.org/speakers/dickshya-gurung

SOUTH AMERICA

Maracaibo,
Venezuela

Alirio Romero

From: Maracaibo, Venezuela
Current City: Madison, WI

> "I WANT TO HAVE A FUTURE, AND THAT'S SOMETHING I CAN'T HAVE IN VENEZUELA. I REALLY WANT TO DO SOMETHING IN MY LIFE."

In Venezuela, I lived in a beautiful town called Machiques. It has about 65,000 people and is surrounded by mountains. I grew up there with my parents, two brothers, and many, many close relatives. It was normally a little bit dangerous but I was really small. I think my life was good. My parents owned a farm where they raised dairy cows and sold the milk. We lived in a house in Machiques, and my father traveled to the farm every day. My mom was an elementary school teacher. My two brothers and I had a pretty normal life. I have really great memories of times I spent with my family. We have a huge family, 50 people in total, and all my grandparents, uncles, aunts, and cousins all lived in our small town. I remember we were always getting together with all of the family, almost every week. We would cook traditional food and eat together. Another really important part was the music. We loved to dance and play music. Our family parties were really fun. I actually learned to play the guitar and spent many hours making music with one of my cousins. I finished the school there in Venezuela.

In 2009, the government told my family that they were going to take away his farm. That didn't happen until 2013. Then, our life changed a lot, and my dad didn't have a job without his farm. Other things were getting bad in Venezuela. We couldn't always find the food we wanted. Life got more dangerous. People were getting robbed or even killed when they went out. We had to stay inside more and be careful going out anywhere. My dad was so upset about losing his farm that he was ready to leave and never go back.

A long time ago my father's sister had moved to Wisconsin and was living in Janesville. So, one of my older brothers went to visit her and decided to move there. He liked it and is still living in Madison. When things got bad in Venezuela, we all talked about what to do, and my family decided to move to-

57

gether to the United States. We talked about it a lot. We had visited here before, and my father wanted to find a new place for us to live that would be safe. We decided that we could be safe in Wisconsin. We got ready to move, but one of my brothers stayed behind in Venezuela. I know he wants to come here, and I hope he can do that someday.

Leaving my home in Venezuela was a hard time for me. I was really sad because I was leaving my friends, my family, and my girlfriend. I felt like I lost everything, and needed to start all over. We arrived in Miami and stayed there two days, and after that we came to Chicago, and my brother picked us up. It was so great to see him because we had always been very close, and I hadn't seen him in years.

We arrived in February 2018. When I arrived in Madison, I had mixed feelings. I was sad about all I left behind, but I was also hopeful because I want to be someone. What I mean is I want to have a future, and that's something I can't have in Venezuela. I really want to do something in my life. And I didn't want to be all the time just thinking about it. So, what can I do? I just wanted to do something.

The first days in Madison, it was really boring because I didn't have anything to do. I didn't go to school in the first week. I mostly just slept. And I played something like PlayStation with my brother. We went outside, we went to the park, went out to eat, and it was sad because everything seemed so different. But my brother helped me get used to the changes, and I was glad about that.

After a week here, I started going to school. It was great. It was different—really, really different. So, I needed to try to do my best. So, I did, I tried my best in my classes, and it felt good. I met a lot of people, and now we are really good friends, so I am really happy with that. I have some really nice classes, even hip-hop studies. I'm in a club for Latino music, and we meet at lunch on Wednesdays. Our club is going to perform at the annual Latino Festival in April. It is one of the biggest and most popular school dances, so I think it will be a lot of fun. So, my life now is that I go to the school all week and am just free on the weekends. I also work at a pizza restaurant. I've learned a lot of English there. I usually work twenty-five or thirty hours a week.

I am also in an orchestra on weekends on Saturday mornings. My instrument is the clarinet, and we play all kinds of classical music. I've met a lot of great people there, and I really enjoy being part of that group. My cousin goes there, too, so we really like being together. It is nice to be at the university campus and around many different musicians. Music is the one this that is very similar here and in Venezuela. I think it's the same because it's orchestra, so it's classic music. There's only a little difference. I like pop music. Maroon 5, I like them a lot. Currently my favorite song that I am playing on the guitar right is called Romance. I don't know who wrote it because it's anonymous. But it's classical music. I'm pretty sure I want to play that, if I have a guitar here.

I am in my senior year, so I will be graduating soon. I want to go to college, maybe for engineering. I'm super interested in civil engineering, but I also would love to study music or math. I'm thinking about doing the liberal arts transfer program at Madison College so I can keep studying English and other subjects, and then transfer to the University of Wisconsin after two years. But I honestly haven't decided yet, so I will continue to think about the best choice.

I want a calm and peaceful life with my family and friends. I really appreciate all of the opportunities that are available here and want share my love of music to more people. In the future I would like to have a family and *quiero ser tranquilo* ... I want to be at peace.

VIDEO LINKS

greencardvoices.org/speakers/alirio-romero

AFRICA

Nairobi, Kenya

Edman Ahmed

From: Nairobi, Kenya (Somali)
Current City: Madison, WI

> "I HAVE 6 BROTHERS AND 4 SISTERS. THE OLDEST ONE IS 24, AND THE YOUNGEST ONE IS 7, AND I'M THE FOURTH YOUNGEST. FOR ME, GROWING UP IN A BIG FAMILY WAS CHAOTIC SOMETIMES, BUT IT WAS PRETTY GOOD BECAUSE IT WAS NEVER LONELY."

My name is Edman Ahmed, and I was born in Nairobi, Kenya in Africa. From what I remember, it was pretty good because I was fortunate to go to school. In Kenya, education wasn't as common as it is in America. Not all kids were able to go to school. I'm from a big family—I have six brothers and four sisters. The oldest one is twenty-four, and the youngest one is seven, and I'm the fourth youngest. For me, growing up in a big family was chaotic sometimes, but it was pretty good because it was never lonely. I always had someone there for me all the time, which is a great attribute of big families. I got to see most of my family every day. It was really good to live with my grandmas and grandpa. We had a happy life together.

I remember on the weekends I went to Quran school where they taught us Arabic and about Islam. During the week I went to a big private school with many of the friends I had since elementary school. We had a lot of fun there, but we had to do a lot of stuff there, too. We learned English, Swahili, math, reading and writing. But my parents didn't think the educational system there was good enough for us, so they decided that we should move to America for better opportunities for a good education.

My parents were born in Somalia, but my brothers and sisters and I were born in Kenya and the US. We had basically the same background but with many different languages. I grew up with language of Somali from my mom and dad and Swahili in Kenya. During school we spoke mostly English but sometimes Swahili. I was always pretty talkative. I had to code switch a lot. Many days I would use two or three different languages, so when I came to America, it was easy to switch to English at school and Somali or Swahili at home. I feel lucky to have this language capability because I think it will help me a lot in the future.

When I was in second grade, I moved here and it was pretty crazy. On the first day we got to Madison, it was snowing. That was the very first time I had ever seen snow. I was surprised how different Madison was from Africa. We had a uniform for the private school in Kenya, but here people can wear whatever they feel like. When we started public school here, it was a little weird for me because I had to wear different clothes every day. It was kind of hard to get used to after always wearing a uniform.

Another memory of my first day in the United States: I remember coming into our new house, and everything was so different. My new house compared to my house in Kenya was smaller. But a good thing was that in America we had many more neighbors. That means more friends for me. Also, I was closer to my school, John Muir Elementary School, so we could walk to school which was really good.

Since the education was different, I had to get caught up with what other students had already learned. Their way of speaking, their language, was kind of different because the pronunciation in Africa was different. But it was alright because I had already studied English. So even though my accent was different, we could at least communicate. I speak English with my mom and dad and my brothers and sisters, along with the other languages, so I keep many aspects of my culture, which is good.

We moved around a little after we got here, and I went to different schools. Now I'm at Memorial High School. Kids from all the other schools I went to are also here now, so I get to see them all the time now. I'm a freshman, and it's pretty good. I knew a lot about the school because my middle school's right across from it, so I went there a lot, and my siblings came through here. They told me stories about it, like where to go and stuff like that.

I've gotten used to high school, and I like all the different classes I can take. I was accepted into a Pathways Program where I can learn specifically about health careers. I was also accepted into the People Program, which is a way to increase my chances of being accepted into the University of Wisconsin. If I get accepted, I will have free tuition, which would help me follow my dreams. I started in the People Program in middle school, and they have helped me understand what I need to do and make sure that I have the requirements to get in, which is a handy resource to have. During the summer while I am in high school, I will get to live in the university dorms for like a couple of weeks while I take summer classes. This will help me get used to the way of college life to make an easier transition from high school to college.

On the weekends I volunteer at a food pantry in Verona, Wisconsin, which is a small town near Madison. It's a place where we organize food donations and we help make sure all the donated goods like food, soap, baby products, and things go to the families that need them. And we help them pick out the right stuff and pack it up for them.

My dream, or what I want to do when I grow up, is being in the medical field or the law field—like a place where I can help people every day and basically always make a difference in other people's lives. I would love to find a job where I could help not only the people in America by also anywhere in the world. Right now I am a freshman, so I have three more years of high school. Through activities in my Scholars of Color Club, the People Program, and the Health Careers Pathway, I hope to work hard enough to go to college and get a job where I can help people, one person at a time. That is my ultimate goal in life.

VIDEO LINKS

greencardvoices.org/speakers/edman-ahmed

Manali, India

ASIA

Tenzin Rangdol

From: Manali, India (Tibetan)
Current City: Madison, WI

"I ALWAYS KNEW ONE DAY WE WOULD MIGRATE TO THE UNITED STATES. MY FAMILY WAITED FOR TWELVE YEARS TO BE ABLE TO COME HERE. AT LONG LAST WE GOT A CHANCE TO COME HERE. THE PROCESS WAS VERY DIFFICULT."

I was born in Manali, India. It is a high-altitude Himalayan vacation town in India's northern Himachal Pradesh state. Many people come to Manali from southern India because all year long there is snow, and the mountains covered with snow are so beautiful. It is very cold in the winter as the elevation is 6,726 feet. My parents used to own a shop selling sweaters and jackets to tourists. My grandmother had started the shop, and later my parents took it over. They really enjoyed working there. My family lived in a house near the shop.

My family consists of my mom, dad, younger sister (Tenzin) Namdol and me (Tenzin) Rangdol. In my Tibetan culture we are given names from the monastery when we are born. They give the parents a piece of white paper which always says "Tenzin." So my sister and I are both "Tenzin," but we always go by our last names so she is Namdol, and I am Rangdol.

I began going to a school called CST Manali School, specializing for children from kindergarten to fifth grade. After third grade I moved to Suja TCV, and I went there from fourth to tenth grade. Both schools are run by the Central Tibetan Administration, North India. My sister also went to CST Manali School. We learned how to play Tibetan musical instruments. Also, the physical education teachers taught us how to play baseball, which I really liked a lot.

In India I finished eleventh grade. That school had more than a thousand students, and many of them were friends of mine. I miss them so much, and they probably miss me, too. It was really hard for me to leave them. In India after tenth grade, we need to choose our career. There are three main schools: one for lawyers, one for business and economics, and one for scientists. There are also vocational training schools for cooking or baking or other things like that. Because I wanted to be a computer programmer, I went to a school for scientists.

I always knew one day we would migrate to the United States. My family waited for twelve years to be able to come here. At long last we got a chance to come here. The process was very difficult. My dad traveled nine times to the capital city of India, New Delhi. We just waited a lot, and when the visa provision was going on, I was in school and taking the class ten final board exam. After I was done with my exam, the school gave us a one-month holiday. So, I was very comfortable. The visa preparation was finally over, and we got the visa before I had to go back to school. In New Delhi my dad had a very good friend who used to live upstairs from us. He actually had a lot of money and was better off than we were. He helped us a lot during the visa preparation process. We really appreciate all that he did to help us.

When the day to move arrived, I was excited. We all were excited, but we were also scared. We knew that many problems can happen on the airplane. We had heard of crashes, hijackings, etc., so sometimes while we were traveling here, the sadness would get worse, and I would be scared. There were a lot of moments like that. But once we landed, it was so great. When I came out from the airport, it was so good. I was feeling so good.

In India there were so many dogs and policemen. But when I came here, I didn't see anything like that. It was so good. The biggest difference I found when I first got here was that the culture was so unlike what I was used to. Making conversation was so hard. I didn't know what to say or how to say it. We had to get used to how to shop in the big shopping malls because we had never seen those kinds of malls before, and we also had to learn how to take the buses because we didn't know where anything was located in Madison. Luckily, we were used to the weather. The weather here in Wisconsin is very similar to the weather in Northern India—we almost always had snow in Manali.

Now I'm living in my uncle's house. I'm glad to have him because he cares about us so much and really has helped us a lot. He helped us get settled in our new schools—my sister is in middle school, and I go to high school. The James Madison Memorial High School is really good. I made some friends here from Mexico, Venezuela, and Nepal. I take two different English classes. I am reading books for thirty minutes every day. I speak a lot to my family to learn better. After school my little sister and I often ride our bikes to our neighbor's basketball court to play basketball. We have a lot of fun doing that. I really love to play basketball, and I love to watch basketball, too—my favorite team is the Golden State Warriors.

I am learning other things about the culture here in the US. The Thanksgiving culture is so awesome. My school served Thanksgiving for eighty students, and we all ate turkey and other traditional foods. I really liked the mashed potatoes. Shopping is very different here. I think the sales of Black Friday are awesome too. I have also learned many things about American football because my uncle always watches his favorite team—the Green Bay Packers. It is fun to watch football with him because he is so excited, and he explains the game to me too.

About fifteen miles from Madison there is a Tibetan temple called Deer Park. There are many Tibetan families who live in or near Madison. My family goes to Deer Park for special events. His Holiness the Dalai Lama visits the temple. My Tibetan culture, religion, and the language is still alive because of His Holiness the Dalai Lama who went to India from Tibet when the Chinese occupied our country. I am grateful for all that he has done. It is so good to see so many other Tibetan people when we go to the temple.

When I was in India, I had wanted to become a computer programmer. In America we can choose to be whatever we want. I have one more year of high school, and I will study very hard and improve my English because now I want to go to a university to become a dentist. When I was a kid I broke my teeth many times. To get them fixed it cost more than the monthly income of my parents. We were very fortunate because a dentist always helped me without cost. Even though he helped me so much, I still have horrible teeth, and I refuse to smile with my teeth. I want to make people smile. If I become a dentist, I can help other people be happier with their lives. One smile can make one's day different.

VIDEO LINKS

greencardvoices.org/speakers/tenzin-rangdol

Ana Fernandez Roque

From: Puebla, Mexico
Current City: Madison, WI

"I'M ALSO TRYING TO LEARN A NEW LANGUAGE BECAUSE I FEEL IT WILL OPEN MORE DOORS FOR ME...I REALLY HOPE TO...SHOW PEOPLE THE THINGS ABOUT MEXICO THAT I LOVE."

My life in Mexico was really great. I lived with my mom, my dad, and my younger sister. First, I went to elementary school. I went to a school that was bilingual, so I learned English there. Then I went to a Catholic secondary school. The girls were separated from the boys, which gave me the opportunity to make deep friendships with girls. All my family lives in Puebla, Mexico. It was always a family-raised environment. I have grown up with a lot of Mexican culture—the food and traditions. My family went every weekend out. We had a lot of traditions. We always had Christmas with my whole family. My grandparents took all of my family to pick our own Christmas trees. We also tried to go to church all of the Sundays.

I have a lot of friends from Mexico—my childhood friends are still my friends. We were in class together every day, so we really built a great friendship. Also I had my family really near me, so if I needed to talk to them or someone to help me, they were always there. It was really special because I know I have many people there that I love and who love me.

I remember the time I realized I was coming to the United States. My sister's and my education is really important to my parents. They wanted to try to send us in a program to either Canada or the US so we could practice English. My parents really wanted to do something different, so my Mom found an opportunity for the whole family to come to Wisconsin. She said, "This is a great opportunity because we can all go and you can practice your English." So we went to the embassy, and we did a lot of paperwork. And it happened, so that's why we're here. I remember we were so happy because we really wanted to practice our English and learn about another culture.

I came in the summer, so we didn't have school. I was fifteen years old. I was really sad to leave my family, but I wasn't thinking about the sadness because I was so excited. I got into the airplane, and then we came. First we did a layover in Texas, and then we came to Madison. When we first came, it felt like a vacation. It felt really exciting and new. We stayed in a hotel for a week, and then we found an apartment. I was really excited—it's really different. The weather was so hot. Where I lived before in Mexico wasn't that hot.

Then the school started. I was really thinking that it was going to be like in the movies. What was really hard for me the first day was that in Mexico I already had a lot of friends from my childhood, so I didn't have to look for anyone to be with at lunch. Here I felt sad at lunch because I was alone. I had to start all over again and start looking for new friends. So I just looked for some girls that I thought were nice, and I had lunch with them. I wanted to talk to new people. At the beginning, although I knew English, it was really hard because I was speaking English 24/7. You think you know it, but when you get here... wow. I knew English, but I was translating everything in my mind. Now I feel confident, but at the beginning it was a little bit nerve-wracking and hard.

I was so excited to come to the US. I wanted to experience myself how the American school was. I also love English, and I think it's really important to be bilingual and learn as many languages as you can, so I was really happy that I was going to come here. The plan was to come first for a year, but then we really liked it so we extended it to three years. Finally, it's going to be five years, so this is my fourth year here.

After these four years in Wisconsin, I have more friends. I think my English has improved. I am trying to do more activities and get involved in more things. For example, I am the director of Mindfulness Club here at Memorial High School. I really like doing yoga and things that are relaxing, so I really wanted to have my own club and invite people to feel calm. In Mindfulness Club we talk about the things that are stressing us out. We color, meditate, are quiet, and listen to music. After we have that time, we feel a lot better, so that's why I really like that club.

I try to be involved in other things, like the Greater Madison Youth Program where we did community service. We went to a house for the elderly, and there was a woman who only spoke Spanish. She was really happy to speak Spanish with me because I understood her when no one else could.

In Mexico you don't work when you are a teenager. We normally work after college. I think one of the best things about being here is that I have the opportunity to work as a teen. I work in Target, and I have been working there for two years. That's really amazing because I now have experience having a job.

I really treasure and appreciate my family, the food, and the feeling of being in Mexico when I am in the US. When I go to Mexico, it's really fun because I get to eat the food that I love and be with my family and friends, so it's really cool. I really miss my favorite food—Mole Poblano. It's the most famous food from my state. It's a chicken dish with chocolate and chili peppers. My family brings me the spice mix for the dish when they visit me in Wisconsin. In fact, my whole family is coming this April to the US. There will be fifteen of us! I can't wait to see them. Every time I see them, I tell them all my stories about living here, and they tell me they are really proud of me. I'm really happy that I had the opportunity to come here.

In the US I learned that being bilingual is incredible. That's why I'm going to Indonesia for three months this summer to volunteer to teach English. The program is to teach less-fortunate kids English so they have more opportunities in the future. I'm also trying to learn a new language because I feel it will open more doors for me. My hopes after Indonesia are to continue traveling. I want to go to Italy and learn Italian because I want to learn more languages.

In the time that I have lived here, I hope to have taught people something useful about me and my culture. Since I have lived here for four years, I feel like a part of me has absorbed parts of American culture. I'm starting to dress up like people here—hah! I want to do more things and go to college, and I absolutely want to come back and visit my friends here. I think this experience is amazing for me, and I really have a big part of Wisconsin in me. I really hope to give Wisconsin something from me, too. I always try to be nice to everyone, help people that need help with English, and show people the things about Mexico that I love. That's what I hope for and what I want to do.

VIDEO LINKS

greencardvoices.org/speakers/ana-fernandez-roque

AFRICA

Mogadishu, Somalia

Juweriya Hassen

Born: Mogadishu, Somalia   **Raised:** Camp Cheddar, Ethiopia
Current City: Milwaukee, WI

> "IT'S NOT LIKE WE WERE HEARING BOMBS; HOWEVER, ETHIOPIA HAS A LOT OF ANIMALS, LIKE LIONS, HYENAS, AND THINGS LIKE THAT...MY MOM DID NOT SLEPT AT NIGHT BECAUSE SHE HAD TO WAKE UP TO LOOK OUT FOR HYENAS."

I was born in Somalia in 2001. So the fighting started in 2003; I was living there, and the fight was not that big. We just lived there, and my mom said we have to go to Ethiopia. And my dad said, "No, we have to stay." So we lost my father; he said, "Well, I will go and get lunch for us," and then he never came back. My mom said we had to go. In 2007, I remember the last night I was there—it felt like the house was like moving us. Bombs were exploding when we were sleeping, and my mom just came and said we have to go. We slept outside, and that was our last night there. So all the money we had we gave to our father, and he just never came back, so we didn't have the money to fly from Hargasa to Addis Abbaba. So we just took a car, and that's the way we left Somalia for Ethiopia.

Life in Ethiopia was a lot harder than in Somalia. It wasn't very safe. It's not like we were hearing bombs; however, Ethiopia has a lot of animals, like lions, hyenas, and things like that. We didn't have any house there; we just had clothes that we put together and lived inside there (in the clothes we had). My mom did not slept at night because she had to wake up to look out for hyenas. When we had to go to the bathroom or take food from the UN, we had to walk two and half hours to get over there. If you need breakfast, you have to wake up at 4:00 in the morning to get there at 6:00 a.m. and come back. It took two hours. You had to go to sleep earlier in the night so you don't feel hungry. The United Nations gave us food at 6:00 p.m., and if we stayed up until 9:00 at night, then you'll feel hungry but have nothing to eat. So you have to go to sleep quick just like that. It was hard. I was living with family—with my sister, my brother and my mom.

We were in Ethiopia for nine years. The last year, they said, "You're going to the United States." That was 2014. We felt like . . . excited. We didn't

73

feel sad that we're leaving family or friends. We were just happy, and we would say, "And now we know where we'll be—where we're going to grow up." It was so nice—it was a dream. We didn't know anyone here in the US. We were just alone. Nobody helped us get here.

When we came from Ethiopia, we moved to Marsa, Egypt. Then we came to New York. Then we came to Wisconsin. There were three flights. It was amazing. We just were happy, not sleeping on the flights. We were just looking around and saying, "Where's the United States . . . where's the United States?" We were just waiting for the social worker. We had to have his help to get home. He went shopping with us and showed us how to do laundry the first time.

When we came here, to Milwaukee, everything was difficult. You get your hopes up, and it's nothing like that. We go to school, and we get on the bus, and we get everything. We get food here. When we were in Ethiopia, we didn't know where we were going to eat at night. Now we have everything. Everything is good. When we first landed in Milwaukee, a man from the government—I don't know his name—took us home. He was telling us everything about the United States, and he was helping us. He told us, "This is a better place, and you will like it. And if you need any help for social security and anything else, then I will help you. And you will feel free."

Being in the US, it was my first time to see White people. In Africa everyone was the same. When we came here, the interesting things were that we had a lot of food in our house. And we have a clean house and safety and everything. And when you open the door you see around you everything is clear and clean. Nothing is going on: you don't hear anyone yelling. It was kind of amazing. The weather was difficult. It was the first time I saw snow.

When I was young, I never thought I would go here and do something like this. I will go to school, and I will be what I want to be. I hope that when I grow up I will be a lawyer. So I still need to study to be a lawyer. I want to be a lawyer because a lawyer is helping a lot of people. It's a different world. I don't know what kind of lawyer, but I just want to be lawyer, and also I want to make money. A lawyer makes money, and also it's kind of like a successful person and classic. You are an important person if you are lawyer in government. I'm working hard to be what I need to be. I'm going to study law in college. I haven't thought of which college I want to go to yet.

Currently, I live with my mom, two brothers and five sisters. Four are older than me, two are younger than me, and one is my twin. When my mom is working, my two big sisters go to work, and I take care of their two babies if mom is not there. I am kind of like a mother. I'm kind of like cooking or cleaning or taking care of the kids. So nothing's fun. Outside school we don't do anything because my mom is very protective. So I have to go to school and then home—nothing else. So when you go out, you can't go anywhere else. In school my favorite subject is math. I like math, but when I don't understand it, I actually hate the subject but I do like math, and school is helping a lot.

VIDEO LINKS

greencardvoices.org/speakers/juweriya-hassen

NORTH AMERICA

Michoacán, Mexico

Alain Quezadas

Born: McAllen, TX   **Raised:** Michoacán, Mexico
Current City: Milwaukee, WI

> "THEY STOLE OUR OTHER CAR...MY DAD WENT AFTER THEM. AND THEY SHOOT MY
> DAD WITH A GUN. MY DAD CRASHED AND DIED."

I was born in McAllen, Texas, but as soon as I was born, we left to go back to Mexico. I grew up talking Spanish with my big family. I was with them all the time, and I would go out with my friends in Mexico to eat and cruise around and go to the park. I did activities after school, like dance, and I played a little bit of volleyball. I lived with my mom and my siblings and my pets. I have four dogs—all chihuahuas—in Mexico. I want to see them soon.

I went to kindergarten for three years. I learned Spanish, how to draw, and read. Then I went to elementary school. I went for six years and learned math, science, and how to read in Spanish. I also had English class, but it wasn't so good—it was the basics. Then I went to middle school for three years and that was a fun part of my life. That's when I would go out with my friends after school. We'd go to eat, make things, and cruise around my town—that kind of stuff. I went to dance academies in Mexico, and I dance Mexican dances with friends. It was fun because we were so good at dancing.

My mom told me that I was going to move to the US since my sister came here to study. I think because my sister was here first, I thought it would be fun. I would be here with my sister, and she would probably help me in school, other things, and stuff. I came here with my uncle. He is a truck driver. I first stopped in McAllen, Texas, and then I went to San Antonio, Texas. From there we flew to Chicago, and, finally, I got here to Milwaukee, Wisconsin. The journey was fun because I wasn't the truck driver, and I was with my sister and cousins. We were all playing and talking. The trip to here was not boring. I felt kind of sad because I needed to leave my family and move to the US.

I came to the United States, but I didn't have a passport. I only had my birth certificate. I work so hard to have my passport now because my mom is in Mexico, and I am with my sister. I went to Texas with my sister to obtain my passport and a card that says something like, "I give permission for my daughter so that she can have my passport." And it was harder because I lost my dad in Mexico because of the violence. I needed the death card and that stuff and the translated card. I had to do all that stuff, and it was so hard to get my passport and lots of papers and things.

I've been in Milwaukee for four months now. It was fun at first when I came because I met my aunts and my cousins who live here that I've never seen before. I like it. It's different because it's not like my home in Mexico . . . it's different. I was worried that if I didn't know her, it would be like, "Who are you? You're in my house, but I never see you." But we are more close now. My first day here, I went downtown with my cousins, and my first week I went to my cousin's quinceañera. And after that we went to Wisconsin Dells to go camping and that kind of stuff. It was fun, so fun.

When I came here, I started school one week after. At the start it was a little bit difficult for me to make friends with people who do not speak my language because I'm not so good at talking in English. It's not so good. Like, I can't express myself like I want to do, like in my language. After school I go to the academy of dance two days a week, and on the weekends I go to my family's other houses to be with my cousins. I want to finish high school, and afterwards I want to be a doctor, like a surgeon doctor. I want to have good grades and only As in my report card and in my transcripts because I need to get a scholarship for college because my mom can't pay for my college. I want to have a scholarship so I can study at college and finish and be a doctor. I want to be able to help and save lives. I want to be a surgeon doctor because I like watching the show Grey's Anatomy, and I like that. I want to have a family. I always wish for an Italian or German wife because I love Europeans.

I want to say, in Mexico the situation is good, but it's so much violence. Where I lived there's drug dealers like that kind of stuff. In Mexico they stole our car when we were working in the farms. There were so many trees, fruit trees. I was present when they stole our car. They came with large arms, and they shoot into the air. They only said, "Give us the cars!" They took our only car, and it was scary. I thought, "What can I do in this situation?" I was with my mom and brother and other people. We gave up. Especially when they said, "Stay over there and give us the car," I was so nervous and said "Okay."

I lost my dad because of the violence. Later, our other car got stolen. I was in my house. My brother was washing the car, and they came with a gun and said to my brother, "Give me the car." Then they go, and my dad went after them, and they shoot my dad with a gun. My dad crashed and died. My dad died because of the violence. And the government, they didn't do anything, like they are blind. They have blame. They didn't do anything about it.

I want to say, "*Saludos a todos, a toda mi gente bonita en Italia mis amigos de alla.*" Also, to all my friends and my mom, I love you. I want to see you soon. Thank you all for giving this opportunity to share my life, my situation, my immigrant story.

VIDEO LINKS

greencardvoices.org/speakers/alain-quezadas

ASIA

Quetta, Pakistan

Bibi Sadeeqa Sulaimankhel

From: Quetta, Pakistan (Afghani)
Current City: Milwaukee, WI

"IN MY COUNTRY HOLIDAYS WERE REALLY GOOD, BUT HERE IT'S NOT SO GOOD. IN MY COUNTRY THERE WAS MY GRANDMOTHER AND GRANDFATHER, AND EVERYONE WAS TOGETHER. HERE WE DON'T HAVE ANYONE."

I was born in Pakistan, in Quetta, and my life was really good. I lived there for thirteen years. My life actually was not that good but a little bit good. I love Pakistani things, like their dresses and jewelry. When I was in school, there were classes like here, and there were also classes where we learned about Islam. We were a little bit poor, and my dad has a problem, and so we came to America.

We flew from Pakistan to America, and we landed in Milwaukee. It was our first time on a plane. I was nervous. We had no family in Milwaukee. It was only us, my mom and my father and five sisters and three brothers. After two years I got new brother, so now I have four brothers. For the first two to three months, we just went to school, and later we found some other Muslims that spoke our language, and we had like a new family. At first we only found one other family to be our friends and that was all. For one year we didn't find anyone, but now we have a lot more friends from Pakistan, and we also have friends who are our neighbors. Some of them are Somali friends and Karen friends. I learned from my friends that Islam is important, that our religion is important, and that family is important.

When I came to Milwaukee, I started going to the Story School. The school was very good; I liked it. Then I came to Pulaski High School. I started in ninth grade. I'm currently in eleventh grade. My favorite subject is math. On the weekend I help my mom, and I when I get homework, I just work on my homework. I do my chores after school and on the weekends.

When I came to America, the biggest change was the house and the weather. We came in the summer. The was no snow or rain, and summer was very hot. We went shopping. The people in my country, we'd never seen Black people and tall people. The stores were different, too. The money was different. We could buy things with just one dollar. Pakistan didn't have a one-dollar bill.

There was only a five or a ten. Chocolate would be like five or ten. It's much cheaper here.

In my country holidays were really good, but here it's not so good. In my country there was my grandmother and grandfather, and everyone was together. Here we don't have anyone. When I with my mom, she would tell me stories about what happened to her when she was kid, and I would laugh. I don't have any other friends to spend celebrations with. There is only one other family from Pakistan in Milwaukee. Some of the holidays we celebrated were Eid and weddings. There was lots of family back home. I have a very big family. In my house there were ten people; in my grandmother's house there were more than fifteen; and in grandmother's sister's house there were more than twenty. There was a lot of food at holidays. Weddings would last for five days.

My two brothers and my sister just got engaged. My first brother will be married after two years, and my second brother will wait until after his fiancée graduates from high school. My sister's fiancé wants to get married in six months, but she wants to wait a year. Everyone my siblings are engaged to are in Pakistan, and I hope they marry soon so we can go to Pakistan and celebrate. The weddings will be amazing. On the first day of the wedding, we get friends and family together and go to peoples' houses to invite them to the marriage. The next night we put henna on the boy's hands and celebrate with his family. The next day the boy's family goes to the girl's house and take the girl back with them. After a couple hours everyone comes to the house to dance and drink tea. Then the boy and the girl sit together and give each other sweets, like cake. On the last day the girl gets ready and sits in the living room, and her mother gives her lots of gifts to give to her new husband's family. I'm excited because everyone will dress up and eat good food and dance and be happy.

I like puppy dogs. I like to play with the dogs. I like Hindi songs and Spanish and English songs too. I like to know how to speak Spanish and Farsi. I love Hindi movies and Pakistani and Hindi dramas. My American teachers are good. Miss Contreras, Miss Corsetto, Miss Millan are my favorite teachers. I like them because they're good, and any time I have problems, I go to them. They help me out a lot. When I have good news, I share the news with them. My favorite thing to study is math. I also like my gym teacher, Mr. Martin. I like to play volleyball with my best friend, and I like watching soccer. Ronaldo is my favorite.

In the future I have a few goals: to be a nurse or join the army. I'd like to be in the army to help poor people and save them. I'd also like to be a teacher or a stewardess. With that job I can travel to new places like India. I want to see Indian actors and actresses.

VIDEO LINKS

greencardvoices.org/speakers/bibi-sadeeqa-sulaimankhel

ASIA

Sittwe, Myanmar

Aziz Kamal

From: Sittwe, Myanmar (Rohingya)
Current City: Milwaukee, WI

> "BECAUSE WE DID NOT HAVE ANY DOCUMENTS, WE MOVED BY SHIP. THERE WERE A LOT OF PEOPLE IN THE SHIP, AND THERE WAS NOT ENOUGH FOOD FOR ONE MONTH JOURNEY IN THE SHIP."

I was born in Myanmar, the state of Arakan (Rakhine State), the port city of Sittwe. One part of the city was Rohingya and one part was Burmese. The Rohingya people were fisherman, merchants, and grocery store owners. When I was five years old I first went to school, but I could not finish middle school because it cost a lot of money. My family didn't have enough money for fees and school supplies, and that's why I left. I was only in fifth grade. After I left school, my dad moved to Malaysia to look for a better job. After a few years my oldest brother moved to Malaysia, and after a few more years, another brother moved too. In Sittwe, the situation was getting bad for the Rohingya people. My dad helped by sending money from Malaysia. The government didn't allow us to travel to any other cities. It was hard because we could not even visit our grandparents in Minbya. Any travel with ship or car was not allowed for the Rohingya people. If you got a fever, you could go to the clinic and get some medicine, but it was really hard because the hospital was expensive, and because we couldn't travel there weren't other options. Women had to give birth at home.

When I was in Myanmar, the Buddhist people killed Rohingya people, burned schools, burned our house. The entire Rohingya part of Sittwe was destroyed. In 2012 we had to move to camps outside of Sittwe. The camps were from the United Nations. The United Nations also gave each family one tent and so my family all lived in one for six months. The camps were so far away from Sittwe. We could not live in Sittwe. Right now Sittwe is nothing, just ground, because they burned everything—the store, houses, people's homes, everything.

When we were in the camps, we planned to move to Malaysia. Because we did not have any documents, we moved by ship. There were a lot of people in the ship, and there was not enough food for one month journey in the ship. When we leave from the city, Sittwe, my mom talked to the sailor about money to smuggle her, me, and my three brothers to Malaysia, and the sailor said only our family will go on this ship. After a few days, my mom gave money to the sailor, and when we get to the ship, we saw a lot of people. We ask the sailor, "Why you say only our family will go in this ship? Why you take a lot of people?" And they said, "If you won't come, if you don't want to, go back." But if we go back, my mom will lose our money because the sailor will not give it back. That's why we get in the ship, and he drive in the ocean.

A lot of people died and the sailor threw them in the ocean. Finally after one month, we got to Malaysia. When we got to Malaysia, the sailor kept us to one room. We were not allowed to leave the ship. We were in that prison for one week, and they only gave us water. We could not hear anyone, and we could not see anyone after that. They asked about more money, and so my mom's brother contacted them. They said, "You need to give more money. If you don't want to give more money, I will not give your family." My dad had already moved to the US, and he borrow some money from friends and give money to my uncle to give to them. Then my uncle took us from them.

We stayed two years in Malaysia. I was fifteen, and I hoped I would get some education in Malaysia, but I could not because the government did not let me go to school without any documents. When we got to Malaysia, my dad and my two brothers had already moved to the United States. The United Nations called them to come to United States, so they already moved here. My uncle was working the whole day. He could not help us that much. We are in a lot of trouble in Malaysia because we do not know anyone, and we did not speak the language. I was trying to work at the market to sell fruit, but it's less money, and I worked hard a lot of the time. After that, my dad and my brothers were here trying to get us to the United States. They tried. They go into office to tell them about us. We also went every day to US Embassy in Malaysia. They take a lot of tests, ask a lot of questions, and do a lot of DNA testing to see if we are children of my dad or not. After that, the US Embassy decided to send us here. I decided to come here because of education. I could not finish my education in Myanmar. That's why I came here . . . to go to school, to have an education.

We took a plane from Malaysia to Dubai where we change airplanes and flew to Chicago. When we landed in Chicago, the agent came to welcome us. Then we got on a bus and came to Milwaukee. I saw jungle and forest, and I was scared of where we were going. We didn't see any houses or any buildings.

Malaysia has a lot of big buildings, it was different, that's why I was scared but excited too. We get in the Milwaukee airport and my dad and my brothers came to pick us up.

When I saw my brothers, I was so happy. It was summer time, July, and we had no school. My brother took me to tutoring where they are teaching English in a building at Oklahoma and 65th Avenue in Jackson Park Lutheran Church. It's called the Myanmar Learning Center. I went over there in summer, and I met a lot of people who speak our language, and I was so happy to talk to them. But I didn't know English yet—I understood some, but I didn't know how to speak it. After the summer the agent came and took me to the MPS office to apply to the school. At the time, my brother was at Pulaski High School. He was in eleventh or twelfth grade. He said to come there with him. When I came, I didn't know anyone, only my brother. He introduced me to a lot of his friends, showed me how to open the locker, and how to go to class.

I want to be a doctor because when I was in Myanmar, a lot of people died when we lived in the camps. There was not enough water or food—a lot of people died, and there were diseases. My mom said, "Look, there are a lot of people dying, diseases, you have to get an education." I said, "How can I learn?" because the government didn't let us go to school, and if we go to a private school, it's a lot of money. We don't have money. My mom said, "Your dad is in Malaysia. He will call us, and we will go over there, and you will learn." At the time my mom said, "You must be a doctor because you have to save these people."

When I was young, I was excited to be a doctor. After I moved here, I forget everything my mom told me. When I was here, first day of school, one teacher asked me, "You came here and you have the opportunity to do whatever you want." They ask, "What will you be?" I was confused. I didn't know what to say. When I got home and I asked my mom, and she said, "Don't you know what I said when you were young?" I told her, "I don't remember." My mom remembered and told me that when I was young, people were dying of diseases and that I wanted to be a doctor. That's why I decided to be a doctor. That's why I am learning hard in school.

I volunteer every Monday through Thursday from 5:00 p.m. to 7:00 p.m. at night at the Burmese Rohingya Community of Wisconsin. There are almost 200 students learning about Islamic Studies, and I volunteer. I make flyers, translate newspapers, and take attendance in classes. When the teacher doesn't come, I teach the Islamic Studies classes. I translate a lot because I can speak Rohingya, Burmese, Urdu, Malay, and English.

My family has six brothers and one sister. I am fifth brother. I have four older brothers, one younger brother, and one younger sister. When I arrived in the US, one brother was studying in college, and one brother was working. We came here to be a full family again—together again. Before, we were separated—some were in Malaysia, some in Myanmar. When we are here, we are full family, everyone in one house, and we are so happy. After one year of being in the United States, my oldest brother has married, and he has one son and one daughter right now. We do fun things like watching TV together, eating traditional food together, going outside and going to picnics. Last year we went to Wisconsin Dells and to the zoo in summer.

VIDEO LINKS

greencardvoices.org/speakers/aziz-kamal

ASIA

Kamarmaung, Burma

Moo Eh Paw

Born: Kamarmaung, Burma (Karen)
Raised: Mae Ra Moe, Thailand
Current City: Milwaukee, WI

"MY OLDER BROTHER GOT MARRIED, AND HIS WIFE DIDN'T WANT TO COME TO THE US. THAT'S WHY HE STAYED BEHIND...I WAS REALLY SAD, BUT I COULDN'T DO ANYTHING."

I was born in Burma, and I was living there a few years, when my parents decided to move to Thailand. I was five or six years old. When I heard this, my dad told me that Burma was not a peaceful place, and the Burma soldiers want to kill the Karen people, so my parents decided to move to the refugee camps. We moved to the refugee camps, and I lived there ten years until I was fifteen or sixteen years old. I went to school there and studied there because I love school. I want to make a better life for my family in the future. I lived in Thailand, and I have four siblings—three brothers and one little sister. I went to school every day, like Monday through Friday. On Friday nights I used watch movies and play with my family and my friends and my brother and sister. I didn't do anything else. When we lived in Thailand, it was a little bit hard for us to find money to pay the education bill, so my parents decided to come to the US.

When my parents decided to move to the United States, we had to go interview and to get a shot. We had to do the interviews three times, then the last interview, we had to come to the Mae Sot. If we pass, we can come here. And if we don't pass, we can't come here. At that time my older brother got married, and his wife didn't want to come to the US. That's why he stayed behind. He still lives in the refugee camp. I came with my family—my little brother and sister and my parents. That's all. When I was leaving, before I came here, I felt sad because I had to part with my brother. Our family loves each other. My brother would take care of me sometimes, and even though he got married, he never forgot us. At the time I was really sad, but I couldn't do anything. I still keep in touch with my oldest brother. He calls my mom sometimes, and we talk. He talks mostly to my mom, and sometimes we say hello. He talks about how he wants to come here, but he can't do anything about it. Before, his wife didn't want to come to the US, but after she thought about it, she does want to come. But they can't because they need permission from the government. Before we left I said goodbye to people—all of my friends and family. I was a little bit sad.

I remember on the plane ride—I had to take a plane in Bangkok going to Doha in Qatar. Then, a plane to Chicago. And then from Chicago I came here to Milwaukee. When I came to Milwaukee, it was on the bus. The entire trip took two days. The first moment here was a surprise because I'd never seen the tall buildings—like beautiful buildings. I'd never seen something like that before. It's really a surprise for me. I think it was special because in my life I never used to live in a place like that. That's why when I got to Chicago, I felt like I wanted to go back to Thailand because I don't know to speak English, and I was scared of the tall buildings. That's why I wanted to cry. I wanted to go back. I didn't want to come to here. It was very difficult for me.

There were a lot of differences from here and Thailand. The food is different here. The water is different—if you want hot, you can open it hot, or if you want cold, you can open it cold in the sinks. And the bedroom is different—the rooms were more bigger. I have a room by myself, but usually I like to live by myself so my little brother and sister don't bother me. They are so noisy. My little sister is five, and my little brother thirteen, and my other brother is seventeen.

The first day here . . . it wasn't good. Like it was bad for me because I didn't know anyone here, just only my cousin. My cousin came before us, so we already had family here. He came to the US seven months before we did. Sometimes on the weekend I go visit my cousin, and sometimes we go to the lake and just walk around. The first day I came to the school I felt sad for a whole month. I was kind of scared because I didn't know how to speak English—that's why I wanted to go home. I feel all the time I told my mother I want to go back to Thailand. As the months passed, I wanted to learn English because I want to learn more languages. I'm doing my best and giving my best to study. Then after a few weeks I got more friends, and they come talk to me. Some people are Spanish, and some people are Burmese, and some people are Karen. I got a lot of Karen friends because I don't know other languages.

In the evening or on weekends, I want to read a book, and if I'm bored I just listen to music and just play with my family. Sometimes I play soccer with my little brother. I usually listen to K-pop, BTS and GOT7. My favorite food is fried chicken and sushi. My favorite movies are Korean movies and Chinese movies. On the weekend I just visit my cousin and take care of my niece and nephew. I play with them. I don't have anything else to do.

I want to go to the university or college and get a better education for my future. I want to study social work because I want to help other people in refugee camps. Whether it's an adult or a little kid, it doesn't matter for me because I just want to help people. It's good for me. I want to go to the University of Wisconsin-Milwaukee, I'm in twelfth grade and will be graduating May 21, 2019. I'm excited to graduate. English is my favorite subject. After I graduate high school, I will go to the University of Wisconsin-Milwaukee. I want to learn more languages like Korean, Japanese, Chinese.

VIDEO LINKS

greencardvoices.org/speakers/moo-eh-paw

ASIA

Adirampattinam, India

Shaheed Dhawheed

From: Adirampattinam, India
Current City: Milwaukee, WI

"MY FAMILY IN INDIA IS SO HUGE. I WAS SURROUNDED BY GOOD PEOPLE. MY RELATION IS MORE THAN TWO THOUSAND PEOPLE...THEY OFTEN TOOK CARE OF ME. THEY LOVE ME. AND I LOVE THEM."

I was born in India. The town was called Adirampattinam. My life was awesome. My family in India is so huge. I was surrounded by good people. My relation is more than two thousand people (aunts, uncles, nieces, nephews, my grandmother's and grandfather's siblings and their children), and I can't count all of them. A funny word to describe it is "infinity." I know everyone else all around the town. Most of the people were from India. They often took care of me. They love me, and I love them.

I have two siblings, one brother and one sister. I'm the youngest in my family. My brother is twenty-five, and my sister is twenty-one, and I am sixteen. When my sister had a wedding, there were like more than a thousand people. We invited a thousand people, and approximately 800 came. It lasted a week. We decided to put her wedding into a hall, but my sister didn't want to do it in a hall, so we just did it in our home. They had a religious marriage. There is a thing called *nikkah*—it is a way of marrying. All the people we invited to the wedding came for breakfast and lunch that day.

My childhood was half and half—sometimes I had good things, sometimes bad things. My kindergarten time, my school days, they were horrible. The teachers didn't care about the students. They didn't do their best, and sometimes the teachers slept in the classroom. When the teachers slept, some of the students went outside to play some outdoor games. One thing about Indian school, whenever you get something wrong, you have a punishment, and they beat you. They hit you hard, and it's legal in India, and it's common.

In India we played a lot of games. There's a traditional game called *Kabaddi*, and it's kind of like dodgeball without a ball. There's another team on the other side, and you have to touch them on their side, and you have to get back to your side without being tackled. We played a lot of marbles, and we played a

95

lot of soccer (football to the rest of the world) in our country and another game called Cricket. Cricket is set up exactly like baseball, but the rules are different. Soccer and Kabaddi were my favorite games to play.

My father is a US citizen. He got a US citizenship by naturalization back in 1995. I was born in India, and also I got citizenship. Then my mom decided to get me a nice education, so she asked my father to get me from India. He was living in the United States at the time but coming to India for vacation. I was waiting for my passport for two years. Moving to the United States was so sad. I miss my whole family. It's just my brother and me in my home. My dad used to be here like five months ago, but he went back because he likes to stay in India. I just miss them. I'm lonely all the time because I miss them, all of them.

When I first came here, I was like speechless. I didn't speak to anybody. As time went on, I learned to speak English. I was like a silent person, but when I came to school, I tried to speak with classmates, and they tried to speak with me too. After a few months past, I developed my language and now I just communicate with everybody. I have just been here like a year, but every other English as a Second Language student is shocked by me because I speak English better than they expected me to. When they struggle to do their homework, I help them do it sometimes.

I studied in two different schools—one was an elementary school, which is also known as a "matriculation school" in India. I studied there from K-2 to fifth grade. After I finished my elementary school, I moved up to a high school that was only for boys from sixth to ninth grade. I have a lot of friends over there. It was a fun time when I was with my Indian friends. You might wonder why I'm studying in boys' high school—it's because of the ethical restrictions that we have. In my hometown the teenage male and female students have to study in specific schools for their genders because they aren't allowed to be close with the other gender. I don't have any female friends in India except cousins and relatives, and sometimes it is boring without having any female friends. Now I have a lot of female friends because Pulaski High School is for everybody and depends on their age not their gender.

On the weekends I do a part time job. I work as a server. I like my job because I get a lot of tips. I used to work on school days, but I am working right now on weekends. Sometimes I play video games or make music. Right now I'm a DJ and music producer—I do both. I do a lot with music; I have my YouTube channel, and I just post music. Everyone loves my music. I like to produce dubstep, future bass, EDM, hybrid trap, trap music, progressive house, deep house, moombahton, and big room. I just make my music and send it to my friends. I didn't want to post it at first, but then my friends forced me. They gave feedback to me like, "You have to change this one," and then I would change the music, and it will sound good.

When I was in India, I wanted to be a mechanic. But now that I'm here, I think about the future, so I've changed my mind. I'd like to be a DJ and an electronic engineer in the future. I like to do both. I try to take risks. It's complicated to think about it—you have to choose one path. Maybe I can DJ as a passion and be an electronic engineer as a career. We will have electric cars in the future—we won't have petroleum cars anymore, so I don't want to be a mechanic. I want to go into electronic engineering.

In the summer we are planning to go to India because my mom wants to see me face-to-face as soon as possible. I can't go right away because of school, that's why we planned for summer. After, I will come back to the United States again and begin to study. I like the United States, but I like to see my family. I was stuck in between. I'd like to stay here, but I want to see my family. I like the way of education here and the society and the atmosphere. As you can see in India, we found a lot of pollution, and there's people still that have a lot of problems. I like America a lot more than India.

VIDEO LINKS

greencardvoices.org/speakers/shaheed-dhawheed

NORTH AMERICA

Managua,
Nicaragua

Najaris Hernandez-Martinez

From: Managua, Nicaragua
Current City: Milwaukee, WI

> "I REALIZED I WANTED TO BE A DOCTOR LAST YEAR...BUT BEING AN IMMIGRANT AND A FIRST-GENERATION STUDENT, IT FELT LIKE A REACH...NOW I HAVE AN ALMOST FULL RIDE TO MARQUETTE, AND I'M GOING TO MAJOR IN PHYSIOLOGICAL SCIENCES AND EVENTUALLY GO ON TO MEDICAL SCHOOL. I'M JUST SO EXCITED TO START UNIVERSITY IN THE FALL."

I was born in Nicaragua in 2001, and I moved to the US when I was four. I turned five years old here. Nicaragua is not a big country—it's really small. It's in Central America, and right now it's going through political issues. At the time of my birth, there weren't any major political issues—the economy wasn't good, but right now there's political unrest.

In Nicaragua I lived with my mom and some other family in the capital city, Managua. Occasionally we would go to the countryside to visit my grandma. Nicaragua is mainly known for its scenic volcanoes. The geography is really diverse. Going from the countryside to the city is a very different ambience. In Nicaragua you can go to the beaches and you can go out. You can go hiking and volcano sliding. I really like going to the beach there. It's about an hour or two away from Managua. I went to a school called Inmaculada Concepción. I went my K3 through K4 years, so I don't really remember much. I just remember it was a private school.

My grandma moved here in the 1990s. First she moved to California and Miami, and then came to Milwaukee because the living expenses were high. Then, after I was born in 2006, she brought me and my dad over so we could have a better future. I think I found out I was leaving for the US the day before I left, so I was really unprepared. I didn't really know what was going on. I just remember waking up, and my mom was like, "Well we're going to take you to the airport." And I'm like, "Why? Why am I going to the airport?" And she was like, "You're going to go live with your grandma and your dad, and I'm going to stay here." At the time, as a child, you don't really understand, "I'm moving away forever; this is absolutely going to change my life." Especially when it is from a third world country to a more developed country. I didn't really understand, but now I do—it had a really big impact on me.

I remember that my mom was really sad about me leaving. You know, as a child you can't really comprehend. On the plane, I was was asking my dad a whole bunch of questions like, "How are we flying . . . How is that physically possible?" I couldn't understand. Growing up you don't really notice the absence of not having your mom in your life until you get older. It was really hard to go back to my roots and understand where I came from, especially since I didn't have a lot of people like me surrounding me.

I didn't go to school immediately because I came here in February. I started school, K-5, in September. I remember coming here, and it was really cold—Nicaragua is always like eighty degrees or a little bit warmer, like ninety; it's in the eighties to nineties every single day. It was just different. My skin was so dry, and I wasn't used to wearing lotion. I was just like, "Why is my skin so dry?" The food was different—it was still like Hispanic food but not like my country. It's mostly like Mexican people and Puerto Rican people here, so the Hispanic people that I interacted with weren't from my country, and it was just a different experience. The first couple of days I was mostly inside with my family, but in Nicaragua you're always doing something outside. It was just different to be inside because it was so cold, compared to being in my country where we were just out and about.

I now live with my mom, who came over about three years ago. I've been living with her the past two years. It's kind of different when you grow up without your mom, but now it's just normal living with her. There are all these things we just didn't experience. I would go over to Nicaragua during summer and spring break, but it was just not enough time to develop that mother and daughter connection that we now have. Now I guess I'm just a regular teenager here. I'm in twelfth grade, and in the summer, I'll be starting school at Marquette. The summer program is to help me get a head start and transition from high school to college. I'll also be taking a couple of college classes. I really like school. I want to be a doctor because when I went back to Nicaragua last year, I saw that there were a lot of health issues, and I want to give back to my community. I want to give back through healthcare because I saw that my family didn't have good access to healthcare in Nicaragua or even here in Milwaukee.

I moved to Pulaski last year as a junior, and it was really different because I used to go to a school that didn't offer many things, so when I started at Pulaski I played volleyball, and I did track. I did an apprenticeship in medicine at the medical college where I was able to shadow doctors, talk to many physicians, and take part in labs. It helped me solidify that I did want a career in medicine and helped me get some experience in the field. I also have a job. It's just mostly little things to help me prepare for my future. On the weekends I like to go out downtown to eat with my friends and my family.

I realized I wanted to be a doctor last year, and it was like, "Okay, now I'm going to have to make that effort." But being an immigrant and a first-generation student, it felt like a reach. I thought at the time, "You're reaching to have a big dream such as being a doctor." But I sat down and thought, "Well, I haven't been really doing that bad in school. If I want it, then I should go for it." Now I have an almost full ride to Marquette, and I'm going to major in physiological sciences and eventually go on to medical school. I'm just so excited to start university in the fall.

Right now Nicaragua is going through a big political crisis, and it's not really getting talked about. It's similar to what's happening in Venezuela, and there are things that aren't brought to the media that are very important and should be getting coverage. My family members tell me that everything is okay, but there are occasional kidnappings and murders, which shouldn't be happening. People are getting killed just because they voice their political opinions. I don't think that's okay. I was going to go back for winter break, but I couldn't because there's so many bad things happening right now. I really miss it though. I really miss my country, and I want to give back one day. I know that I can't be the only one to change things, but I want to push for economic change and get people to think about their situations differently. The people have to make an effort first and not rely on the government for a better quality of life.

VIDEO LINKS

greencardvoices.org/speakers/najaris-hernandez-martinez

ASIA

Sittwe, Myanmar

Annuwar Hussein

From: Sittwe, Myanmar (Rohingya)
Current City: Milwaukee, WI

"SO, HE WENT TO THE POLICE STATION TO REPORT WHAT HAPPENED. THE POLICE DIDN'T TAKE ACTION BECAUSE THE POLICE WERE FROM THE SAME RELIGION AS THE PEOPLE WHO STOLE STUFF FROM THE SHOP OF MY DAD."

I was born in a small town in Arakan State in Myanmar. There are a lot of different religions in Myanmar: Buddhism (Burmese), Islam, and Hindu. The government didn't give opportunities to Rohingya Muslims. The government was and is only helping and giving opportunities to Buddhist and Hindu people.

I have a big family in Myanmar. My parents had six sons and one daughter. My dad had a big pharmacy shop since he was thirty-two years old. He sold medicine and had a very successful business. But the Buddhist people didn't like it if Muslims were getting progress in life or business.

One day five Buddhist people came to my father's shop to buy something. One person bought something, but the other four people stole some of our stuff. My father saw when they stole. He told them, "Give me back my stuff!" but they didn't give it back. Instead, they bullied and argued with my father. At that time my father did not have a phone to call the police. So, he went to the police station to report what happened. The police didn't take action because the police were from the same religion as the people who stole stuff from the shop of my dad.

After a few days, the Buddhist people came to burn down my father's shop when the shop was closed at night. Then the police people came to arrest my father because his shop was burned. The police didn't help my father. My father told them what happened when he was in the police station, but the police didn't do anything to the Buddhist people.

After a few hours, my mom went the police station and paid some money and took him out from the police station. My parents were very upset because my dad lost his business. My parents could not do anything because the police and the government support the Buddhist people but not any other ethnic group.

My mom said, "If we stay here, we will get into more trouble. It's better to leave this country and move to another country." My dad listened to my mom, and he moved to Malaysia, a majority Muslim country. There he met a person, and they became friends. The person helped my father a little bit. He needed to find a job, and he got a job. But he had to work a lot, and he got little money. He could not apply for a higher job because he didn't have Malaysian citizenship and any document paper or any proof to be able to work. He just worked a lot and got little money and sent the money to my mom so my mom could support us. My oldest brother went to high school. When he finished high school, he decided to go college. After two years of college, he decided to move to Malaysia because my dad was there already. When he got there in Malaysia, my brother stayed with our dad. He also didn't get a good job. It was too hard to find higher job in Malaysia for other people, but it was easy to find higher job for those who were born in Malaysia.

After a few years, my dad went to UNHCR, explained his problem, and asked for help. At that time the UNHCR people said that they will call my father later. They called him after a week and said, "If you want to go to the USA, you can, but you have to wait for two years or more." When he got information about the possibility to go to the United States, he called my mom and told her to come to Malaysia because he wanted everybody to be able to come here together. "We will have documentation, so it will be better to find a job and live in America," he said.

We traveled for one week to get to Malaysia. When my mom, three brothers, sister, and me got there, my dad had already moved to the USA. My dad said that we had to wait for six months, and we said, "Okay we'll wait six months." After three months, the office said we had to wait for almost two years, and after two years we can come to USA. Because we already came to Malaysia, we could not go back in my country. So, we said, "Okay we'll wait two years."

When I was in Malaysia, I tried to apply to school, but I couldn't because I didn't have citizenship. So instead I applied for a job, and I got a job as a motorcycle repairman. I worked there almost two years. While working there, I got a lot of experience. I can repair anything that has to do with a motorcycle. After two years, we got information to come here, and we did. When we got here, me and my siblings went to school, but we didn't know that much English. Because my dad had already come here, he helped us a lot with everything.

When we came here at first, we were so happy because we were reunited with my dad. We were separated for a long time. In the USA our family is finally all together.

My dad already rented a house before we came, so we all stayed together at home. My dad sent me to high school in ninth grade. I didn't know how to speak English, and I took ESL class that year, and I was so confused at first. When I came in the school, I didn't know anything, and I didn't know anybody. Then one student introduced himself and spoke my language to me. He helped me a lot by showing me how to check my schedule, open my locker, and go to class. I was so happy because I got a friend.

At first, I went to class, and after class I went home. I didn't understand anything. After two months I spoke English a little. After two years I got auto engine class, which is my favorite. I didn't understand a lot of English. Math class is my favorite subject. I understand math more than other subjects because in Burma I had learned a little bit of math already. I have experience doing mechanical handywork. My auto engine teacher taught me a lot. I was so happy, and now I am a senior. After I graduate, I plan to go to college because I want to be a good mechanic engineer. I chose an automotive major because that is my favorite, and I have a lot of experience about it.

My parent tell me, "You can do what you like, that is your choice, but you are to be famous in your future. You have to focus and be successful in your future. In America you have a lot of opportunity; you can do anything you want." I visited a lot of colleges in junior year, and I saw a lot of different colleges. I like a lot of colleges, but some of them are so expensive. I chose Gateway Technical College because it's not that far from my house, and they have my program with automotive studies. If I chose another college, it would be too far from my house, and some of colleges don't have automotive program. Last semester I visited the Gateway Technical College campus, and I saw their students working in the auto body shop. I liked that, so I think I will go to that college.

Author chose not to share digital story.

Mae Kaw Ka,
Thailand

ASIA

Htoo Ktray Wah

Born: Mae Kaw Ka, Thailand (Karen)   **From:** Mae La Oon, Thailand
Current City: Milwaukee, WI

"AFTER ALL THE CHECKUPS, WE WAITED FOR ANOTHER YEAR IN MAE LA OON, AND WE HEARD THE NEWS THAT WE CANNOT GO TO US BECAUSE OF A BIG EARTHQUAKE AND TSUNAMI THAT HAPPENED IN JAPAN."

My life in the refugee camp was easy. There was not a lot of work to do at school, but we had school that we had to go to and had to pay for every grade that we attend. But if we fail the grade, we had to pay a lot of money that we can't afford. So, some of us didn't go to school. And the food—it was hard to find food. They give you food for the month like rice, bamboo to make a house, and coal to cook your food. My grandparents are farmers, so they also grew some vegetables. They planted food like squash and beans and sugar cane. I lived there with my mother, father, brother and sister.

I was born in Mae Kaew Ka camp. I moved to Mae La Oon camp when I was two years old because my parents said that people in the northern Thailand don't like Karen people because they take their jobs, and so that's why they moved to Mae La Oon. It was hard to get out of the camp because it was not our country. If you wanted to get out, we had to ask for a permission to get out. The jobs were hard to find.

I didn't know we would be going to the US because my father got us registered when we went to the Mae Sot for a medical checkup. After my dad told us we were registered for the resettlement, we figured out it was for us to go to the US. I remember we had the health checkup, to see whether we have diseases or not. After all the checkups, we waited for another year in Mae La Oon, and we heard the news that we cannot go to US because of a big earthquake and tsunami that happened in Japan. That was in 2011.

We waited for three months in the camp in Thailand, and we came back and stayed there for one week. Then we went to the capital city of Thailand, which is called Bangkok. After that we went to a hotel, and we waited for two or three hours. Then we went to the airport. We were supposed to go from Thailand to Japan the first time, but then the tsunami happened. When we left for the second time, we went to Germany. We walked in a group with other people—I don't know who they were—but they were looking at us. I was embarrassed because I was little, nine years old. I don't remember much. We went inside the airplane. I didn't think it was an airplane because it looked different, and I'd never seen one before. When we rode the airplane, it was hard. It was in up in the sky; we never rode anything before, and when I had to use bathroom, I didn't know where it was or where to look for it. I didn't know how to ask. We didn't get any food on the plane. They gave us one cookie, and that was it. We were really hungry.

When we arrived to Michigan, it was night. We went to an apartment, but we could not sleep because we missed our home. I was crying a lot. I was the first one who cried in the family. My parents were very sad too, especially dad. We didn't have any other family. When we went to school, there was no Karen people, and I didn't speak English, so I didn't talk to people. I had to sit by myself and eat alone. The most surprising thing for me was when we went to the grocery store. It was big. There was a lot a food. It's not like Thailand and the refugee camp. The cashier that takes our money scans our food differently. When we saw snow for first time, it was cool.

Our only relatives live about thirty minutes away in car. We didn't have any other family that live in apartment building with us, and no other Karen people. There were other ethnic groups, but no Karen people. That's why we decided to move to Texas because there is large Karen community living in the area around Austin, Texas. We went to Texas by car. We stayed for five years. Texas is a state where I have close family and where we can live together. When we moved to Wisconsin, it was because I have four to five relatives from my father's and mother's sides. That's why we moved to Milwaukee. We've been here for two years now.

I'm in eleventh grade now. I like English class because it's easy. We read stories, and we don't have to solve problems like math or science. I like to go to this school because I have Karen friends here, and I can make new friends that speak the same language as me. I came to school this school two years ago when I was in ninth grade. After school I stay for College Possible for two hours, and then I go home. I don't have a part-time job. I want to go to the University of Wisconsin-Milwaukee when I graduate from high school.

I would like to travel to Korea—that's the only place I like. When I would watch K-drama, that's where I want to go the most. When I first time came here, I didn't know about anything. When I start watching a South Korean television series called *Dream High*, I started to like K-pop and Korea, and I still like it now. I like the music the most. There are a lot of bands I like. I like their dancing style and their sound of the song and their voices. I like how their dance powerful, and I like their voices.

VIDEO LINKS

greencardvoices.org/speakers/htoo-ktray-wah

ASIA

Hakha, Burma

Uk Lian Thawng

From: Hakha, Burma (Chin)
Current City: Milwaukee, WI

"IN THE FUTURE I WANT TO BE AN AUTO-MECHANIC. I LIKE FIXING THINGS THAT ARE BROKEN...THAT'S MY PASSION. AND IT'S FUN FOR ME."

My name is Uk Lian Thawng, but some people call me "Tta Lian" as a nickname. I have three siblings—one brother and two sisters. My brother is currently sixteen; my middle sister is fourteen; the youngest sister is eleven, and I'm eighteen. I remember a lot of things from when I was in Burma. When I was young, like ten years old, my dad left me alone. I was alone because he had to go to Malaysia to get work to have a job a better job. I was crying that time; I was young. After that I lived in Chin (Hakha) for two years, and my father sent us money. After that he said he would call us and tell us when we can come to Malaysia with him too. And then I was so happy.

I didn't really want to go to Malaysia, but sometimes I thought, "It's going to be fun." And it was really fun there. Everything was fine and fun. But I didn't want to leave the Chin (Hakha) because I had fun there and didn't want to leave my friends. But I really had to go to Malaysia, so we went to Malaysia. I saw my father, and he was like a stranger. Like I didn't really recognize him. We lived five years in Malaysia, and then after that we came to the US.

So when we came to the US, we rode a plane. I really couldn't wait to ride a plane because I never had before, but I didn't like it, and I didn't want to leave Malaysia again. Like some people went to the US, and I was jealous. My friend went to the US, and I just felt jealous. But when it was my turn, I didn't really like want to go to US because Malaysia was so fun. I had friends there, and I didn't know about the US yet. I didn't feel like I wanted to go, and then I had to go and in airplane! I didn't think that was fun: my ears hurt, and it was a long time ride in the airplane—about seven hours. Then we arrived in Chicago. In Chicago we rode an airplane again to Kalamazoo, Michigan, and then my family, which was my dad's cousin, picked us up, and we went to our new home. I felt uncomfortable because the house was small and dim. I shared

111

a room with my brother, but I don't really like sharing a room.

We arrived in the night, so they didn't show us anything at first. After two weeks went by, they showed us houses, and we went to a buffet, which was my first time. They also showed us what America looked like, but I didn't go to the downtown. It was pretty fun. I was interested in how different America is than Burma, and it's so interesting for me because I've never been in a place like this that is kind of a popular country. I can drive a car, and I can do whatever I want, and it's freedom. I have big plans, and a big future.

The first place I lived in Michigan was Battle Creek. When I first went to the school, I didn't know anything. I had one friend, but he didn't really help me, and I felt so bad because I wasn't doing well in school. I didn't talk a lot in class. I felt so bad, and like I didn't want to go to school that much. I didn't want to talk in school, but they wanted me to me talk, but I couldn't speak English at all—just a little bit. After that I started in seventh grade in the middle of the year. After that I went to eighth grade, then ninth grade. I did well in ninth grade, and I knew that my life is getting better.

Last year in summer 2017, we moved to Milwaukee. I have more fun in Milwaukee than Michigan. I tried to go to Alexander Hamilton High School, but they said they have a lot of students; they had no more seats. Finally, I applied to Pulaski High School because my cousin told me to. He said they try to be strict, and they are rich now, and I was like, "Oh that's a great idea," and I moved here. It's better than I thought.

My dad wanted to live in Michigan first because his cousin is in Michigan, and then he said, "We won't move anywhere. We won't move no more." And then I was like, "Okay, that's fine." And my mom was like, "there's more jobs in Milwaukee." She said, "Michigan is like a village, small town. It's not that popular." My mom has three cousins in Milwaukee, and the three of them said, "You guys can move to Milwaukee, so whichever is better for you guys." We agreed, but my dad disagreed. My uncle picked us up with a U-Haul, and we moved to Milwaukee with my whole family, and we got better jobs.

Over the summer, I joined the soccer team, which is varsity soccer, and when the season ended, I joined College Possible. I stay after school and go to College Possible sometimes just two times a week. On the weekend I just play video games like *Fortnite* or *Apex Legends* and chill with my friends, hang out with friends, and go outside. I also like to go eat at a Korean restaurant. That's my favorite. I like listening to music, like rap and hip-hop and sometimes country songs.

Basically, in the future I want to be an auto-mechanic. I like fixing things that are broken. I like auto repair. I want to study mechanical engineering in college. That's my passion, and it's fun for me. That's my hobby. And I have a plan for that, and I have a big future for that. After high school I want to go to Milwaukee Area Technical College (MATC) for two years and then continue at the University of Wisconsin-Milwaukee (UWM) for the other two years.

VIDEO LINKS

greencardvoices.org/speakers/uk-lian-thawng

ASIA

Maungdaw, Myanmar

Nur Fatema Nor Bashar

From: Maungdaw, Myanmar (Rohingya)
Current City: Milwaukee, WI

"MY MOTHER AND ME TRAVELED TO MALAYSIA BY SHIP. IT WAS SO HORRIBLE BECAUSE OVER ONE HUNDRED PEOPLE WERE ON THE SHIP, AND WE DIDN'T HAVE ENOUGH ROOM OR FOOD. BUT WE WERE PATIENT BECAUSE OUR DESTINATION WAS TO GO TO MALAYSIA AND BE WITH MY FATHER."

My name is Nur Fatema. I was born in Maungdaw, a town in Rakhine State (Arakan State) in the western part of Myanmar, very close to Bangladesh border. At the time I was the only daughter in my family. When I was five years old, I asked my mom, "Where is my father"? My mother replied he was in Malaysia. I asked again why he didn't live with us. My mother explained to me, "When your father lived here, the police and military forced him to work without earning any money. One day he went there to work, and the police and military gave him a lot of work to do. If he couldn't work, the police and military would beat him." After that I no longer asked my mom why my dad moved in Malaysia.

The situation was getting increasingly hard for us in Myanmar. My mother's father, my grandfather, and his family fled to Bangladesh. So, my mother and I followed him and also fled to Bangladesh. We were traveling with all the Rohingya people that were fleeing and escaping to Bangladesh. We stayed in Bangladesh for six months. At that time I had contact with my father. I told my father we wanted to stay with him. My father did hard work in Malaysia. He gave money to us and asked us to join him in Malaysia. My mother and me traveled to Malaysia by ship. It was so horrible because over one hundred people were on the ship, and we didn't have enough room or food. But we were patient because our destination was to go to Malaysia and be with my father. I was eight years old at the time. I remember it was a very long journey— going along Myanmar and Thailand, until we got to Malaysia.

I went to school in Malaysia, but I couldn't finish school because of money. I got three siblings while we lived in Malaysia—two brothers and one sister. My father worked hard but for less money. It wasn't enough to feed my family and pay my school fees. I had to leave school, but my dad really wanted me to go to school. It was hard. My father didn't want me to be like him and have no education. My father wanted me, my brother, and sister to go to school. One day we went to the United Nations to renew our refugee card. My father explained our situation to the United Nations people, and they said to my father, "If you decided to go to USA, you and all your children can go to school without having to paying money." And when my father heard that, he decided to come here.

When we first got here, it was so scary because my family didn't know anyone, and we didn't know how to speak English. We didn't know where a store was or where we would buy food. When we arrived, my mother's brother was already here. My mother's brother has a wife and three kids—two girls and one boy. I am best friends with the two girls—my cousins. We live close to one another, too.

On the first day of school, when I came to school, I was excited, and it was scary too because everyone could speak English. I didn't understand anything. But I met an ESL teacher, and the teacher introduced me to two students that I could speak my Rohingya language with. When I saw them, I was so happy and excited. They help me a lot like how to go to class, how to open and lock my locker, and how to get lunch. That day I started to understand my class.

I am so happy right now as I have both of my parents here with me. My family has seven people in total now: my father, mother, two brothers, two sisters, and me. One brother is nine years old, and my sister is eight years old. They both go to Alexander Mitchell Integrated Arts School. My other brother is four years old. He's not going to school yet. I got a brand-new sister in Milwaukee. She is so cute. She is three months old. I love her so much. I am playing with her every time I am in the house. Sometimes I am helping my siblings with their homework. I also help my mom with cooking. We prepare Rohingya food which consists of rice, fish, chicken, vegetables, milk, and chilies.

Only my father is going to work. My mom stays home with my little sister and brother. My dad makes envelopes with machines. He works very hard.

There are a lot of Rohingya people in Milwaukee, and we speak the same Rohingya language. For Eid and Ramadan, people visit each other in their homes, and we eat together. While the celebrations are the same, it's different. Cooking is the same, but the food tastes different. In Malaysia all food was very sweet; in Myanmar it was spicy; here the food is different, too.

I have been here for almost two years now. For almost two years I am a student, studying and still attending Pulaski High School. I am eleventh grade right now. I want to study more and more. I like English class and art class the most. I want to be a nurse in the future, but first I want to learn how to speak full English.

Aziz, my Rohingya friend, who is in this book with me helps me a lot with translations especially. His English is very good, and he helps all the people.

VIDEO LINKS

greencardvoices.org/speakers/nur-fatema-nor-bashar

NORTH AMERICA

Guánica, Puerto Rico

Chadier Figueroa Feliciano

Born: Yauco, Puerto Rico   **Raised:** Guánica, Puerto Rico
Current City: Milwaukee, WI

> "I WANT TO BE A POLICE OFFICER BECAUSE I JUST LIKE IT. I'VE GOT A LOT OF FAMILY MEMBERS IN THE POLICE AND IN THE ARMY. MY COUSIN WAS A DOCTOR IN THE ARMY, AND MY UNCLE IS A POLICE OFFICER IN PUERTO RICO."

In Puerto Rico I lived with my mom, stepdad, two older sisters, and one younger sister. I went to the elementary school, María Luisa McDougall. I liked to spend time with my friends. We played basketball and baseball. When I was home, I played video games. Every day it was pretty much the same. My day was usually going to school and coming home. I would ride bikes with my friends, or we would go to the store to get candy. I would come home to eat dinner with my family. My favorite food to eat is lasagna. I would play with my dogs. I had two pit bulls; their names were Maco and Tyson. Then, I would go to bed.

My family celebrates Thanksgiving, Christmas, and *El Día de Los Reyes Magos.* That's on the sixth of January. We play games like Monopoly, cards, dominos, and things like that. It was good when I was young. We play games like Monopoly or cards during holidays. My grandmother always won Monopoly—she was really good at it. We would try to cheat, but she was still too good at it. We played different card games like UNO and Brisca. We would go to my grandmother's house. There was a lot of food like *Mofongo, Pasteles,* and *Guineitos en Escabeche.*

Then my mom, stepdad, and siblings went to the United States. They left me behind, and I stayed with my cousins for about a month. I was alone, and I didn't like it. I remember it clearly—it was September 17, 2014. My mom had come back to Puerto Rico, and she told me, "Oh we're all leaving together. We're moving to Pennsylvania," And I was like, "Okay, I don't even care." When I first arrived in the United States, my aunt, my mother's sister, and my cousins were waiting for me in the airport. We lived with my aunt for a month. She helped find my mom and my stepdad a job. We moved into an apartment above her.

I started going to middle school, and I made some friends there. Pennsylvania was new for me. I liked the cold. I made new friends. When I was little, I didn't have close friends that I would talk to, but in Pennsylvania I made some real friends. I played with them and went everywhere with them. We would go to the movies, and they'd stay at my house. We played video games together, stuff like that. In Puerto Rico I didn't do that—I just played at the school with my friends, but we weren't friends outside of school.

I liked Pennsylvania, but after three years of living in Pennsylvania, my mom chose to move to Florida. I don't know why. I didn't like it in Florida. I was mad, but, you know, I lived with her, so I couldn't do much. We lived in Florida for a year. I remember that I liked learning about construction in one of my classes. My mom didn't like it in Florida, and she said, "I wanna go; we're moving to Wisconsin." I said, "Okay." We moved to Wisconsin in September 2018.

After that I told her that I don't want to move from here. I want to stay here in Wisconsin. She told me she won't move anymore. I like this school, but I don't talk to anybody. I like math and history. My favorite class at Pulaski is algebra. I've got my sister here, and I'm making friends now. I came here before, but just for vacations, and I liked it here. My family came in 2017 for a vacation—we were here for like two weeks. We went to the movies. We played basketball. And we went to see the lake.

I live with my uncle, my cousin, my aunt, my dad, my mom, and my stepdad. My other cousins live together next to us. All my family lives together. Here I don't really do anything—my mom is working . . . my dad is working . . . my aunt's working . . . my uncle's working . . . everyone's working. I just stay alone in my house and play video games. I play *Fortnite*, but I don't play any other games—only *Fortnite, BlackOps,* things like that. I also eat but not with my family because everyone is working. On Fridays we go out to eat together, usually we have Chinese food or McDonald's. Saturdays they just chill, and I'm usually playing video games during the weekend.

I like that there are a lot of places in Milwaukee that I can go and hang out, like around the mall where they just opened a new arcade. There's bowling and ping pong and pool. My favorite is pool. I really love going to Wendy's—it's my favorite place to eat in Milwaukee. I like to ride bikes, but it's too cold to ride bikes now. I like to go around places. I learn about places that I've never been. I like to play basketball when it's not cold, but now I can't, so I like to stay at home and just play video games.

In the future I just want to find a job, maybe go to college, and have a house and a family. I want to be a police officer because I just like it. I've got a lot of family members in the police and in the army. My cousin was a doctor in the army, and my uncle is a police officer in Puerto Rico. I just like it.

I went back to Puerto Rico last year with my mother and stepdad. We went to visit for just ten days. It was for my sister's *quinceañera*. It was a big party. I was her partner, which means I walked her into the party, and we danced together first. I went to different beaches and rivers; I hung out with my family there. I have a lot of family there. We played volleyball at the beach. We also fished while we were there. Hopefully I get to go back again soon.

VIDEO LINKS

greencardvoices.org/speakers/chadier-figueroa-feliciano

Marjida Bi

Born: Mae Tan, Thailand   **Raised:** Singu, Myanmar
Current City: Milwaukee, WI

> "I DIDN'T FINISH MIDDLE SCHOOL BECAUSE OF MONEY. MY FATHER WORKED HARD BUT WAS GETTING LESS MONEY...ALSO, I WAS SCARED TO GO SCHOOL BECAUSE I WAS SCARED THAT SOME PEOPLE WILL BULLY ME."

I was born in Mae Tan Refugee Camp, Tha Song Yang District, Thailand right on the border with Myanmar (Burma). When I was two months old, my family moved to Mae La Camp. My parents are originally from Singu in the Mandalay Region of central Myanmar. Our religion is Islam, but we speak Burmese language.

I didn't finish middle school because of money. My father worked hard but was getting less money. It wasn't enough money for my family. I didn't care about school at that time because I was too young. When my mom sent me to school, I would cry because I didn't want to go school. Also, I was scared to go school because I was scared that some people will bully me.

My father came to Mae Tan, Thailand because of us—to get money. My dad worked hard and sent us money from Mae Tan State of Thailand. After five years he called us to come to Thailand. When I went to Thailand, I knew how important education was in that country. People were talking other languages, but I didn't know which languages they were speaking. Some people were talking Thai and Karen, but I didn't understand about Thai and Karen. When I saw that they are talking other languages, I wanted to learn and understand what they were talking about. So, I wanted to go school and learn more and more education. I wanted to learn the Karen and Thai languages. But I couldn't go school because I didn't have any documents of Thai citizenship. The Thailand government didn't let to go to school without Thai citizenship.

I told my dad I wanted to go to school. He tried, but I couldn't go because I didn't get citizenship of Thai. He decided to move from Thailand. He heard that many people were going to the United States and are getting the United Nations' help. He went to the United Nations' office, and he asked about that. They said to my dad to choose what country he wanted to go to. They gave a list just for him. We couldn't go with him at first because we didn't get the slip. After he got that information slip, many people told him that the US education is the best for your children. So, he decided to choose the United States, and he came to the US. He worked hard at a meat processing plant cutting meat, and he sent money to us.

After three years, we got a letter to come to the US. We told that to my dad, and he called us to come to the US. When we left Thailand, we cried so much because we were leaving behind so many family and friends. We got on a plane in Thailand. We left Thailand, and we had a layover in a Muslim country; I am not sure which one. After one night of travel, we came to Chicago, and then we came to the Wisconsin. When we landed in Wisconsin, my dad was waiting for us. When we saw each other, we were so happy and sad we cried. Then we came to the house. When I got here, I was so happy because I could meet with my dad again. I had not seen his face for three years because he did not know how to work a video call. I love him so much. Also, that day was so cold, and we were fasting for Eid, so we couldn't eat. After a few months, I saw falling snow; I was so excited because I never saw it before. I went outside and took a lot of pictures, and I sent them to my best friends Somaryar and War-hedar back in the refugee camp. They are like my sisters because I only have brothers. They live in Thailand. They were so happy, too, when they saw that I am happy to be in the US. They want to come to the US. The first week in Wisconsin, we went to Walmart. Yeah, we bought a lot of stuff.

My first day of school, I started in ninth grade. I was so nervous. I cried because I saw a lot of people that were not the same as my culture, and they spoke different languages. I was so scared because I didn't know English. I didn't have friends. It was difficult for me to speak English and learn English because English is not my first language. None of the teachers at Pulaski knew how to speak with me in Burmese. But now everything is going okay because I got a lot of friends, and they help me a lot. Now I understand a little bit of English because of them. My family has five people. I have two brothers and me. I have one big brother that works and another who is still in high school. My older brother is a senior at Pulaski High School. He will graduate this year. I'm the youngest of my family, so my brothers look after me. Now I'm still going to high school, and I'm still an ESL student. I'm in eleventh grade right now. When I come home from school, I help my mom. I cook for my family. My favorite food to make is pakapau with chicken or beef, onion, salt, and just a little spicy. When I'm at home, I like to watch movies or cartoons like *Tom & Jerry*.

At night I do homework. On weekends or in the summer, I just sleep, or we go take picnics, watch movies, or help my mom a little bit.

In my future, I want to be a designer. I want to make beautiful dresses. That is my favorite job because I like to fix clothes and I also like to draw pictures of clothes. I know how to sew. Sometimes, I fix some of my clothes. In the refugee camp, I would make clothes for all of my dolls. So I want do that job and I want to get a lot of money for my family. I want to help my family because I love my family. I don't wanna see that my dad is working so hard. Right now, he works at least 12 hours per day.

In the future, I want to be a designer. I want to make clothes. It's my favorite thing to do, I don't know why. I like drawing pictures. I like to make beautiful dresses. I like wearing what I make. I'm also in College Possible. I don't know English very well, but I'm thinking about college in the future.

VIDEO LINKS

greencardvoices.org/speakers/marjida-bi

NORTH AMERICA

Camuy, Puerto Rico

Jonathan Cordero Torres

From: Camuy, Puerto Rico
Current City: Milwaukee, WI

> "I BEGAN TO DRAW AND DRAW AND DRAW. AND IT'S PERFECT. THAT'S MY DREAM— TO BE AN ANIME ARTIST. I REALLY WANT TO DRAW ANIME AND MAKE VIDEO GAMES ABOUT IT."

In Camuy my life was great. It was great everyday, and we would go to the beach, and have fun. We went fishing and went to the carnival. I've never flown a kite though I really want to fly a kite. My father went to the mainland first. It was like, about twenty years he had been there, and he was working, and we called on the phone sometimes. My father has been working. He was good, and he was working in the Milwaukee airport in Wisconsin. When my family went to join him, I was about eleven years old. And we moved into Wisconsin, and we live happy and together. It's because I want to see him again and have a life-time to see him. The reason we came here is because I want to learn the many ways in Wisconsin. The main reason we came was to be with my dad again. It is also a great place to be learning stuff and reading books and creating art.

I remember I took the plane, and we went so high. It was—oh my god! I was kind of nervous when I was leaving. It was me, my mom, and my older sister. The plane was so high I saw a lake, and many people look like tiny ants. We saw the airport, we went down slowly and slowly, and we parked. Later I saw my dad, and I hugged him. I was very happy to see him again. We went to dinner, and we went and eat some ice cream. It was a nice day, to do that.

I have one sister. She is seventeen years old and goes to a different high school than me. She goes to Alexander Hamilton High School instead of Pulaski like me. I live with my older sister, mom, and dad. Sometimes my grandma visits us. She came all the way from Puerto Rico to visit. Sometimes she stays ten days, or it will be twenty days. Sometimes she visits in the summer. She also visits in the winter, usually for Christmas. In the first week I was here it was kind of different from Puerto Rico. I did not know about the ways of Wisconsin, and now I've learned everything. In many ways, it was a lot to learn. I went to school at Longfellow. It still was a hard life here. Making friends was hard. I started Longfellow in 2015. I was eleven years old in middle school, and there were some big kids there too. Then I started Pulaski when I was a freshman last year. I'm in tenth grade now. I was able to make friends a little bit in high school. I was working so hard in school.

On TV I was watching anime, and then I had an idea to create my own anime. I began to draw and draw and draw, and it's perfect. That's my dream—to be an anime artist. I really want to draw anime and make video games about it. I really want to do it, and I'm still drawing all the characters first. Until then I will tell the people to draw the main place. I like all of the anime. *Dragon Ball* is one I've watched recently. *Naruto* was the first anime I ever watched. I don't read manga, but I watch the anime. I just started the first season of *Attack on Titan*. I want to be in anime club; I haven't been to one of the meetings, but I want to. My hobby is to play video game—*Assassin's Creed, Call of Duty*. A lot of people play *Fortnite*, but I never played because I don't have an Xbox, only a Wii U. I play a lot of Mario games. I usually play on the weekends and when I don't have school. I also like drawing and going outside and taking a walk in the park and feeding the ducks; it's fun.

We're still living, our family, but when we went into United States, our dog died. It was really sad, and I was just shocked. I did not know that it happened. We went to United States again and said say goodbye to our family member. I had a pet before I came to the US. It was a dog; she was old, but when I came back to US, for some reason she had a broken leg. It made me sad. She stayed in my grandma's house. She has a dog, too, and a cat. My dog's name was Lilo, and my grandma's new dog is called Lilu. My grandma's cat name is Koala, but sometimes I call her Coca-Cola. I got another pet in Puerto Rico; it's a cat. She's called Peach. She also lives with my grandma. Sometimes she escapes and crosses the street, and it scares me.

Some summers I visit Puerto Rico. When I came to the United States again, the hurricane happened, and I don't know what happened to my cat. I don't know if she died or got in the water or found a new home. It makes me sad because I'm not able to see her ever again. That was my first cat. In the United States I got a new cat. My dad's friend gave me his cat. Her name is Chuchi; she looks like my old cat. Lilo passed away. I was sad when she passed away. The good thing is that she is in my heart, or she is in dog heaven and can walk in heaven and have a doggy biscuit in heaven. After we left Puerto Rico again after visiting, we went high, high up in the plane; then we started to go down, down, down, down until we are in Wisconsin now, and I was really sad when my dog passed away. My life is happy. Our life, it will have a happy ending. One day I really want to have a dog, like a husky or boxer or something. They are cute and adorable and fluffy! They're fun to play with and walk outside and can catch a stick and frisbee. It is a lot of fun.

I want to share something I about dream a lot. What I really want to do is to make my future come true. I keep dreaming about what my future will look like. It's to create anime and video games. It's my life to create these things. I don't understand how I'm going to do it, but I'm still learning how to do it. I want to go to school to study these things. My favorite hobby is drawing pictures or playing with the computer. Arts and crafts is my favorite class. Sometimes I share my art with other people.

VIDEO LINKS

greencardvoices.org/speakers/jonathan-cordero-torres

ASIA

Mae Ra Moe,
Thailand

Ko Mu Ku

From: Mae Ra Moe, Thailand (Karen)
Current City: Milwaukee, WI

> "I WAS FEELING EXCITED ABOUT COMING TO THE UNITED STATES BECAUSE I WILL GET TO LIVE IN A NEW PLACE AND SEE NEW THINGS. I WATCHED 'HOME ALONE' WHEN I WAS YOUNGER, AND I SAW NEW YORK AND ALL THE BUILDINGS, AND I WAS EXCITED ABOUT THOSE."

My life in Thailand was basically: go to school every day and do homework when I get home, if I have homework. Almost every day I played soccer with my friends. We also played *chinlone* or caneball. It is the traditional, national sport of Myanmar (Burma). It's almost like volleyball because you have a net that is about six feet tall, and if the ball touches the ground on your opponent's side, you get a point. You can only use your feet or your head.

I lived with my parents, four brothers, and two sisters. In school I learned English, math, Burmese, and history. After school, I would just go home, do my homework, and then maybe sometimes I went to play soccer and then came back home. To be with all my family, like brother and sisters, is great.

We heard of people that come to refugee camps, and then say, "You want to go to United States? Then you apply for it." So, my family decided to come here to the US. We didn't have opportunities there in the camps like in the United States. We just lived in refugee camps, and then we came to United States.

I was feeling excited about coming to the United States because I will get to live in a new place and see new things. I watched *Home Alone* when I was younger, and I saw New York and all the buildings, and I was excited about those. It all looked new and clean. It was different from the refugee camps. Transportation over there was hard. We didn't have a car, and it took really long to go places because we had to take the bus. The journey from Thailand to the United States was also hard because going to the cities in Thailand was hard because they speak a different language. We had someone who guarded us going from the refugee camp to the airport, so that made the journey a little easier. I think it's pretty exciting, and, at the same time, I was nervous because I'd never been in big city and never seen so many other people like that. I did not know how to speak another language, so it was hard at first.

The first month was great because seeing a new place and eating new food is different from back in Thailand or the refugee camp. In the refugee camps, we didn't have a lot of options with the food, not like in the United States. In Thailand I lived in like a wooden and bamboo house, not like concrete or cement. It's different in the United States. I like living in my house here better. In a bamboo house, you have to replace parts of it every couple of years, so it was a lot of work.

When we first landed, someone was waiting for us, and they had our family name on a paper, and I was excited. Then they helped us to go to the place where we are supposed to live and just showed us the stuff and the house and how to use the stuff in the house. The first week, I just stayed at home, like every day. I didn't really go out. I just went to play outside sometimes with other kids in the neighborhood.

We arrived in the United States over the summer, and I started school in September. Starting school was hard for me. Going to school in the United States the first time was really confusing. It's hard because like I didn't understand the languages and the other people speaking it. There was only like one other person that didn't know how to speak English, so it was really hard. I was nervous. I just wanted to go home because there was no one to talk to—I'm the only one that's speaking my language. It was hard for me. Now that I know a little bit more about English, it's not that hard for me. I can talk to other people, and I can understand them, so I'm not nervous at all to talk to other people, and I am understanding more and more, which is better for me.

My life right now is just go to school, everyday, and learn. When I go home after school, I just do my homework and then play video games. On the weekend I sometimes go out to the park or play soccer. Sometimes I don't really go out—I just stay home and play video games because there's nothing to do. Soccer games are my favorite video games—*FIFA* and then some other games. I like Manchester United. And I like *Fortnite*, too, of course.

The Karen community in Milwaukee is nice. There are a lot of Karen people here. On Sunday we go to church, then worship, and then study the Bible. We celebrate New Year's, and they do the dancing and the singing. Sometimes we invite friends to come over and eat dinner, and we talk about all kinds of things. We eat rice, chicken soup, pork or chicken barbeque, and different vegetables. I don't have a favorite—I like all kinds of foods . . . if it's good, I like it. I have a lot of friends that are from my church.

In the future I hope to learn about mechanics. I want to be an auto mechanic, and I want to learn how to fix cars and design cars. Then, you know, once I know how to do that stuff, I'm going to help my family and my close friends if they have problems with their car.

Right now, I live with only with my mother. My older brother had a family, so he lives in a different house. I also have two brothers that live in Canada. And then I have a fourth brother that lives in Indiana with my father. I also have two sisters—one of them lives in Norway and one of them lives in Canada. They all have their own families. I really want to see them, but we live so far away . . . so it's hard. I want to see them again if I have time.

VIDEO LINKS

greencardvoices.org/speakers/ko-mu-ku

ASIA

Yangon, Myanmar

Mohammad Huzaifa

From: Yangon, Myanmar
Current City: Milwaukee, WI

"AFTER A MONTH, I COULD NOT GO TO SCHOOL IN MALAYSIA ANYMORE BECAUSE I DIDN'T HAVE CITIZENSHIP. PEOPLE WITHOUT MALAY CITIZENSHIP WERE NOT ALLOWED TO ATTEND SCHOOL."

I was born in Yangon, Myanmar. Yangon is a big city. I lived there with my family—my mother, brother, sister, uncle, aunt, and grandmother. I lived there and go to school for four years. I played soccer. I didn't want to go to school because I liked soccer. I didn't care about school because I didn't know it was important. Now I know that school is better than soccer.

From Myanmar I took a boat to Malaysia. We stopped in Thailand, and then we took a boat and a car to Malaysia. My dad went first. He went ten years before we went. My mom, me, my sister, and my brother went to Malaysia to meet him after ten years. The rest of my family came later. He went because it was hard to get money in Myanmar. We left Myanmar because my father hated that he had little money. He went to Malaysia to get a lot of money. My father had a job when he was in Malaysia, but he got only a little bit money, and he could not provide for my family, so he moved for ten years to save money.

I moved to Malaysia for three years, I lived in Malaysia from when I was about eleven. I came with my family—mom, dad, my brother and sister. We all moved to Malaysia. My brother was seven, and my sister was nine. Right now my brother is fifteen, and my sister is seventeen. My second sister was born in Malaysia. She's four years old now. I'm almost nineteen. I'm the oldest of my siblings.

I learned the Malay language. I learned in Malay school for only one month. I went to Muslim school when I was in Malaysia. After a month, I could not go to school in Malaysia anymore because I didn't have citizenship. People without Malay citizenship were not allowed to attend school. But I really wanted to go to school. One day my father told me, "I want us to go in the USA, so you can go to school." I thought to myself, "I can learn all in English. I'm happy here because I can go to school." I was excited to go to school.

We left to go to the USA because it's good for my family, and I can go to school. In Malaysia we did an interview with the UN. They helped us to go to the United States. We had to do the interviews more than one time, maybe three or four times. I don't remember what happened after the interviews. All I remember is my father went to the United States, so my family was all happy because I can go to school. I want to go to school because I want to be engineer. We all came to the US together at the same time. Before I went to the US, I went to school three days because they had to teach me how to go the United States—how to say hello to somebody, how to shake hands, how to say nice to meet you. They taught me in three days. They also taught us how to look in someone's eyes and smile and say, "My name is Huziafa" and say, "Nice to meet you." They taught me like this.

My other family stayed behind. I said goodbye to my uncle and aunty and also my friends. I was feeling sad because I was going to miss them. Going to the US was my first time on an airplane. It was exciting. We were on the plane for maybe two or three days. Malaysia airplane went to Kata airport in Muslim country, but I don't remember the name, and then Kata airport to Chicago airport. After Chicago, I came to Milwaukee on a bus.

It was December 31, 2016. I was very scared because this is a new country, so I was scared because I'd never take airplane. I went on an airplane for the first time, and I was so happy and feeling scared too. A caseworker was waiting for me and my family. I went outside, and it was so cold. I don't like that Malaysia is a hot country, but the USA is so cold. I don't like cold. The caseworker helped my family, my family doesn't know how to speak English, so the caseworker helped me and my family. He took us to show us our new house and how to use heater because I don't know how to use a heater and had never seen heater. It was the first time I ever saw a heater, so they showed me how to use heater. He showed us how to wash clothes and how to open the dryer. They also taught us how to ride the bus.

The first week we went out, it was falling snow, so I took selfie and posted it to Facebook because I'd never see snow. My friend gave me likes and comments. It made me feel happy. My friends were happy for me too.

First time I went to school in the US, I started in ninth grade. I started at Pulaski High School. I don't know English. An ESL teacher, Miss Corsetto, was somebody who could speak Burmese, so she helped me. They taught me how to go class. This school is very big. I didn't know how to get around.

My school in Myanmar is small, and I know how to go find my classes. I was scared—Pulaski is very big. I don't know how to go to my classes. My friends help me find my classes.

My father's friend helped me learn how to go shopping. He took our whole family. He helps us a lot. It was good. It was different. They have a scanner for the food when you buy it. Myanmar didn't have a scanner. Here it is a big market. It was just a store in Myanmar, not a market.

I've been living in Milwaukee for almost two years. I was seventeen when I came to the US. Besides going to school, in the evening the first thing I do after I leave from school is watch a movie. Sometimes I do homework. I go to the gym every day in the afternoon. I usually play soccer at the gym. I tried to join the school soccer team. Now I have a team with my friends. I play defense.

In the future I want to be engineer because I like to fix cars. I want to be engineer, and I would help my family because I'm the biggest son. I want to go to college and study engineering. Math class is my favorite in school now. I also like auto class because I get to fix cars and learn about them.

VIDEO LINKS

greencardvoices.org/speakers/mohammad-huzaifa

ASIA

Vientiane, Laos

Kou Yang

From: Vientiane, Laos (Hmong)
Current City: Milwaukee, WI

"THE FIRST TIME IT SNOWED I, SAID 'OH, WHAT DO I DO WITH THE SNOW?' I WAS COLD, AND I DIDN'T WANT TO GO OUTSIDE. WHEN WE WALKED TO THE BUS STOP, IT WAS COLD, SO MY COUSIN BOUGHT A BIG JACKET FOR ME."

My name is Kou. I'm eighteen years old, and I'm from Laos. I have one younger brother and five sisters, two older and three younger. When I was a young boy, I really feel my dad loves me more than anyone because I am the first son. Where my dad goes, he takes me with him. When I was little, I liked toys, like Power Ranger, and my dad bought them for me. I buy every Power Ranger movie because I like watching Power Rangers. Then everybody called me the Power Ranger as a nickname, because I like too much Power Ranger.

When I was little, around eight years old, I remember that when I stayed with my dad, he liked to take me to go watch the cow fight, and I liked cow fights, and my dad took me to watch chicken fights, and I liked chicken too. I liked my dad so much that where my dad went, I had to go with him. I missed him. When my dad didn't let me go with him, I cried until my dad came back home; then I would stop crying.

When we moved to another city, my uncle came back to Laos and bought my dad a car that my dad used for a taxi. My dad woke up early to take people where they go. He would wake me up, and I had to go with him. Sometimes my dad didn't wake me up. Then I know the plan was like my dad would go, and I had to walk to find my dad. I would ask my dad "Why didn't you wake me up?" And he said, "I go early, and I feel like if I wake you up you would be tired."

My oldest uncle also bought a pond for my family to watch. We had to put the fish in the pond. Around the pond we had coconuts and mangos. We would pick them and eat them. I liked to take my friend from school to go fishing and to eat the coconuts for fun. We go swimming in the pond too.

My grandma and oldest uncle came back to visit Laos when I was two years old. It was the first time I met my grandma. They came to visit again when

I was five, and it was then that my dad said, "Alright, let's go to United States so we can live in the same house. We can be a big family again."

My grandma waited for us to join her in the US for ten years. Then my grandma passed away in 2014. We came to US in 2015. I feel sad about it. "Why not wait for the next year? I miss you so much; the first time I saw you I was only five years old, and I don't remember nothing." My dad had to wait about fifteen years so we can come here. So when we came here, I was like fifteen years old, and I would talk to my cousin and she would say, "I wish you guys had grandma watching you like she watched me".

My dad told me that we will be moving from Laos and go to America to live with my dad's family and to bring our big family together. My dad told me that in Laos he had a brother-in-law and sister-in-law and friends, so we lived in bigger house. We have a better, nicer house. A lot of people ask me, "Why you move to United States? Is your life better? You don't have to work to get food?" My uncle would send money to my dad to buy food and buy rice to eat, and my dad told me, "I don't want to move to United States, but your uncles and your aunties and your grandmother, they want me to go to United States so you can go to college."

I don't like to ride in the car because I get car sick. In Laos I would drive for an hour and had to throw up. So on the day we were travelling to America, my mom scared me and said, "In the car you throw up; in the airplane you will throw up more." When I sat down in the airplane with my family, the sun was rising, and when we arrived in the US, I saw the sun go down. I thought we were back in Laos again. I was just sleeping. My dad's oldest brother, he was waiting for us in Chicago. They had to drive us for two hours. I almost threw up. The car smelled; I didn't like it, so I wanted to throw up.

We're here for two or three days with my oldest uncle, and then my dad's second oldest brother came from Minnesota. He came to take us to Minnesota, and we went to stay there for one month my mom, my cousin, and my mom's cousin, they came to watch us; then my dad brought us. Then they gave us a lot of things, and they said to us, "You guys are so lucky; we give you a lot of things. It's like you are getting married again!" We were over there for one month; then we came back to Milwaukee; then I came to start school here.

The first English phrase I learned was because my uncle told me, "If anyone talks to you, you say 'I don't know' so they don't talk to you anymore." So the first time someone talked to me, I said, "I don't know." I went to school only two years; then my ESL teacher said, "You've been here only two years, and your English is better now." And I said, "I like studying, and I like reading." She said, "Stay here then." I talked to my cousin because he knows English a lot—he's born here, so I talk to him sometimes. Some words I don't know, but some words I know.

The first time it snowed I, said "Oh, what do I do with the snow?" I was cold, and I didn't want to go outside. When we walked to the bus stop, it was cold, so my cousin bought a big jacket for me. The first time I went to school my uncle told my sister the way to go back home, so that day I walked home with her. I didn't know the way, and my sister got lost, and I say, "I don't know the way. Do you know the way?" She didn't know the way, so I thought: where's the house? I remembered a restaurant nearby, so I say, "Oh, I remember this, we go over there. I remember a church, so we go to the church; then turn right, then go straight. My house is over there." We were so lucky. We got home, so I told my mom, "Me and my sister almost got lost." And my mom said, "Really?" And I say, "Yeah." She said, "You get lucky you get home."

My life here, now, I had to take care of my family because I am the only one who has a license, and my mom and my dad don't know how to drive, only I know how to drive. Then I had to take care of my mom, my dad. I like to go any place. I like to go out all the time, we have parties in Oshkosh, so I go there sometimes. Then I had to go there, it was like a one-hour drive. I went to Minnesota like nine times already, and I'm the only driver. It's like a five-hour drive. I take my friend go to Minnesota with me and he said "You're not tired?" I said "I love to drive."

In my free time I like playing games, talking to friends. I like free time because sometimes I go to someplace else—out of town—like to go play with friends. I like friends so much, so I have to go to friends. The first time I go to Minnesota, I took my dad with me to see family. The second time I go to the Hmong New Year in Minnesota. It was fun; I saw a lot of people. People there danced and sang. They wore traditional Hmong clothing. We all played games. The next time I went to Minnesota, I took my friend to go see his girlfriend. Then I drove with my mom, my dad, my sister. I went with three of my three friends the fifth time. The sixth time then I went with my family again. The seventh time I went to the Minnesota State Fair. Then eighth time I went to Hmong New Year again. The ninth time I went to New Year again. I just came back home from Minnesota a couple of days ago. I was there to see family, and I went ice fishing with my cousin.

In my future, I plan to be a nurse. My heart felt like being a nurse, but someone told me that college is harder than high school. In high school I already don't know English really well. I told my dad that I will go in the army, then my dad said, "No, you will not go. Wait until I get another son, then you can go." I said, "Dad, I want to go." My dad said, "No." So I said, "I won't go." I felt like it is the only way I can take care of my family. I have to go work for money, for like pay, for everything. I'm the only one who can drive in my family, so wherever they go I have to take them. If they go to the store I take them. Some days I'm not home so my mom and dad call my brother-in-law to take them. In my future I plan one day to go to Hawaii, China and Japan. In Japan I want to go for the fireworks; they say it's so beautiful. So I want to go. In the future I want to work hard, so we can move to Minnesota and live nearby my family over there.

VIDEO LINKS

greencardvoices.org/speakers/kou-yang

Afterword

Learning from the students' stories featured in this book is just the beginning. The more important work starts when we engage in difficult, essential, and brave conversations about the changing face of our nation.

Immigration plays a significant role in modern US—and our work seeks to build bridges that facilitates rich conversations and understanding. Consider, one in five Americans speak a language other than English at home—what a powerful opportunity for new connections and cultural growth! From classrooms to book clubs, from the individual interested in learning more about his immigrant neighbor to the business owner looking to understand her employees and business partners, this book is an important resource for all Americans.

This collection also includes a selection from our *Act4Change* study guide. *Act4Change* is an experiential learning tool promoting further participation among readers through scaffolded and thoughtful discussion questions and activities focused on hands-on learning. Each activity emphasizes personal growth and knowledge acquisition. The goal is to help teachers, students, and those experiencing our multimedia publications to more closely examine their own stories, while learning about the lives of others.

You can also further engage with your communities and learn more about contemporary immigration through *Story Stitch*, a card-based guided storytelling activity which connects individuals across different backgrounds by encouraging them to share and connect through stories. In addition, Green Card Voices' traveling *state or national exhibits* allow for a visual experience with these and others students' journeys. An interactive presentation, these exhibits feature QR codes that links to students' video narratives, designed to expand the impact of published collection of each personal narratives.

Our aim is to spark deep, meaningful conversations about identity, appreciation of difference, and our shared human experience. To learn more about speaking events, traveling exhibits, and other ways to engage with the *Green Card Youth Voices* stories, visit our website: *www.greencardvoices.org*

Act4Change
A Green Card Voices Study Guide

Each person has the power to tell their own story in their own voice. The art of storytelling translates across cultures and over time. In order to learn about and appreciate voices other than our own, we must be exposed to and given tools to foster an understanding of a variety of voices. We must be able to view the world from others' perspectives in order to act as agents of change in today's world.

Green Card Youth Voices is comprised of the inspirational stories from a young group of recent immigrants to the US, which they've generously shared with a wide audience. This study guide will provide readers with questions to help them explore universal themes, such as storytelling, immigration, identity, and perspective.

Introduce New Voices:
Participants will select one of the thirty storytellers featured in *Green Card Youth Voices* and adopt that person's story as their own "new voice." For example, one participant may choose Vy Luong while another might choose Marjida Bi. Participants will become familiar with the life story of their "new voice" and develop a personal connection to it. After each participant has chosen his or her "new voice," read the personal essay first and then watch the video.

Act4Change 1 :
Answer the following questions—
1. Why did you select the storyteller that you did?
2. What was interesting to you about their story?
3. What do you and the storyteller have in common?
4. What have you learned as a result of reading/listening to this person's story?

Learn About New Voices 1:

Divide participants into groups of three or four people. Provide each group with copies of the written narratives from five selected stories. Each person within each group will read one of the five narratives. Once finished, the participants will share their narratives with the others. Then, as a group, choose one of the five "voices" and watch that person's video.

Afterward, go on to the journal activity below.

Act4Change 2:

Answer the following questions—

1. What new information about immigrants did you learn from this second storyteller?
2. Compare and contrast the storyteller's video to their story. Which did you prefer? Why?
3. What are some similarities between you and the second storyteller?
4. If this really was your "new voice," what might you want to know about America upon arriving?
5. If you could only bring one suitcase on your move to another country, what would you pack in it? Why?

Learn About New Voices 2:

Each participant will be given a third "new voice." Only one can go to each student; there can be no duplicates.

Inform participants not to share the identity of their "new voice." Participants will try to match their classmates' "new voices" to one of the stories in the book. Encourage participants to familiarize themselves with all of the voices featured in *Green Card Youth Voices*.

Act4Change 3:

1. After they are given their "new voice," ask participants to try and create connections between this third voice and themselves. Have the students read their story and then watch the video of their "new voice." Have them think of a piece of art, dance, song, spokenword, comic, sculpture, or other medium of their choosing that best describes their "new voice."

2. Participants will present a 3-5 minute artistic expression for the larger group from the perspective of their "new voice" in thirty-five minutes. The audience will have a template with a chart that includes each of the thirty *GCYV* students' names, their photo, and a one or two-sentence abbreviated biography. Audience members will use this chart throughout the activities to keep track of what has been learned about each voice that they have heard.

3. Ask the participants to describe the relationship between the *Green Card Youth Voices* and themselves:

   a. What did you notice about the form of artistic expression and the story?

   b. What drew you to this specific art form?

   c. Do you notice any cultural relationships between the "new voice" and the piece of art that was chosen?

   d. What is your best advice to immigrant students on how to succeed in this country? State? City?

More than Meets the Eye:

In small groups, have participants read and watch three or four selected narratives from *Green Card Youth Voices*. After that, have group members tell each other facts about themselves and tell the others in the group what they would not know just by looking at them. For example, participants can share an interesting talent, a unique piece of family history, or a special interest. Then have group members discuss things that they found surprising about the students in *Green Card Youth Voices*.

Think about the "new voice" you transformed in *Act4Change 3*. Tell your group something that was "more than meets the eye" from the perspective of that "new voice!"

For the complete version of *Act4Change: A Green Card Voices Study Guide*, visit our website—www.greencardvoices.org

See also:

Act4Change: A Green Card Youth Voices Study Guide, Workshop for Educators
This workshop is a focused learning experience crafted to deepen teacher understanding and provide instructional strategy, particularly designed to be used in conjunction with *Green Card Youth Voices*.

Glossary

Adirampattinam: a town in Tamil Nadu, India located on the coast of the Bay of Bengal

American College Testing (ACT): a standardized test taken by high school students in order to be admitted into colleges and universities in the US

Ama: means "mother" in the Nepali language

Anime: a style of animation with Japanese origins typically characterized by futuristic or fantasy settings as well as colorful images and an action-driven plot

AP World History: a college-level world history course that is taken in high school

Apex Legends: a free-to-play battle royal video game with a hero shooter concept available on Xbox and PS4 consoles

Assassin's Creed: an ongoing series of action-adventure stealth video games developed and published by Ubisoft

Attack on Titan: an ongoing Japanese manga series written by Hajime Isayama that was first published by Kodansha in 2009 and was adapted into an anime television series by Wit Studio in 2013

AVID Student Council: a high school program that prepares students for college and professionalism

Bamboo: a hollow plant with a woody or tree-like exterior grown most often in tropical regions; can be used to create housing, paper, and chopsticks

Battle Creek: a city in southern Michigan in the US with an approximate population of 52,000,000

Big room house: a subgenre of electro house music or electronic dance music

Black Ops: a first-person shooter video game within the ongoing Call of Duty series developed by Treyarch and published by Activision

Brisca (Briscola): a type of Italian card game that involves collecting points by employing tricks and is played by both children and adults all over the world

BTS: a seven member South Korean boy band also known as Bangtan Boys who have won several New Artist of the Year awards for their track "No More Dream" and other high musical achievements

149

Call of Duty: a first-person shooter experience video game that started in 2003 and was originally set in World War II

Camuy: a government-based city located in north-east Puerto Rico with a population of approximately 32,000,000

Caneball: also known as Chinlone, the national sport of Myanmar (Burma); a non-competitive game similar to hacky-sack

Caseworker: a social worker employed by a government agency or nonprofit whose job is to help individuals with their specific, unique needs by providing resources for advocacy, information, assistance, and support

Central Tibetan Administration (CTA): an organization based in India tasked with rehabilitating refugees with education as a primary focus

Certified Nursing Assistant (CNA): healthcare assistants certified to gather and record vital patient information, administer minimal first aid, operate medical equipment, and explain information to patients

Chinlone: (see *Caneball*)

Code Switch: a linguistic instance when a speaker alternates between two or more separate languages in a single conversation

Coding: writing source code needed to create computer programs

Cricket: a popular sport in India that is almost played worldwide; specifically it is a bat and ball game played between two teams of eleven players on a field

Cross Country Running: a racing sport requiring teams to run long distances in open-air, outside courses across various types of terrain; a popular sport in high schools and colleges

CST Manali: a primary school called Central School for Tibetans located in Manali Tibet, run by the Central Tibetan Administration

Culture shock: disorientation experienced by an individual who moves to a new place and encounters unfamiliar cultural and social systems

Dalai Lama: the head of state and spiritual leader of the Tibetan Government in Exile located in Dharamshala, India

Deep house: a subgenre of house music that originated in the 1980s with a combination of Chicago house, Jazz-funk, and Soul music

Didi: means "sister" in the Nepali language

Doha: the capital of Qatar with a population that is approximately 1,800,000

located on the coast of the Persian Gulf

Dominoes: a game played with numbered rectangular tiles that can be traced back to China in the 1200s

Dragon Ball: a manga franchise illustrated and written by Akira Toriyama in 1984

Dubstep: a genre of electronic dance music originating in South London in the late 1990s

EDM: electronic dance music also known as club music

Eid or Eid al-Fitr: a religious holiday celebrated by Muslims worldwide that signifies the end of a month of fasting (Ramadan)

El Día de Los Reyes Magos: also known as 'The Day of the Three Wise Men,' or "Three Kings Days"; a holiday celebrated in Hispanic culture and many countries on the 6th of January; the date marks the culmination of the twelve days of Christmas and the day that the Three Wise Men delivered gifts to the infant baby Jesus; children particularly look forward to this holiday as, traditionally, gifts are exchanged on this date, rather than on Christmas day

Environmental Science: an academic field of study focused on physical, biological, and information sciences

ESL: an abbreviation that stands for "English as a Second Language." These are programs that educate students who speak a language other than English but reside in a country where English is the primary language

Farsi: an Iranian or Persian language with approximately 70,000,000 people using it as their native language

FIFA (Federation Internationale de Football Association): the international governing organization that oversees news, competitions, tournaments, and other aspects of football (soccer) clubs around the world, including the international competition, the World Cup; also a popular video game developed by EA Sports

Fortnite: an online shooter-survival video game

Future bass: a broad genre of music that arose around 2006 that is composed of a variety of sounds and rhythms produced by synthesizer

Garifuna: individuals of African and American Indian descent that mainly live on the Caribbean coast of northern Central America

Gino's Italian Deli: an Italian restaurant located in Madison, Wisconsin

151

GOT7: a South Korean seven member boy band with a debut album Got it? that was number one on Billboard's World Albums Chart, known for their stage performances with a mix of martial arts

Guineitos en Escabeche: a Puerto Rican dish of pickled green bananas

Hargeisa: the capital city in the unrecognized territory of Somaliland in the Horn of Africa, with a population of approximately 760,000

Henna: also called Mehndi; a dye that stains the skin and results temporary body art

Himachal Pradesh State: a state in the northern part of India in the Western Himalayas with a population of approximately 6,000,000

Hindi: one of the official languages of India with approximately 260,000,000 native speakers

Hip Hop Studies: a genre of study that stems from the genre of hip hop or rap music, which was developed in the US primarily in inner city areas that incorporates a diverse local of individuals

Hmong New Year: a celebration for the Hmong people in November and December as a thanksgiving for the harvest season as well as a way to honor their ancestors

Home Alone: an American Christmas comedy film directed by Chris Columbus, produced by John Hughes, and distributed by 20th Century Fox in 1990

Hybrid trap: a style of electronic dance music

Janesville: a city of approximately 65,000 individuals located in southern Wisconsin

John Muir Elementary School: a primary school located in Madison, Wisconsin

Kabaddi: a popular team sport played in the Indian subcontinent with the objective of the game to be for a single player on offence, to run into the opposing team's half of court, tag the defenders and return to their own half of the court without being tackled by the defenders

Karen people: also known as Kayin, Kariang or Yang people who are a number of individual Sino-Tibetan language-speaking ethnic groups, many of which do not share a common language or culture, residing primarily in Kayin State in southern and southeastern Myanmar, making up about seven percent of the Burmese population

K-drama: also called Korean drama; a genre of drama television series created and produced in South Korea

K-pop (케이팝): a musical genre originating from South Korea, originally called Geyo (가요)

Karen: refers to the many Sino-Tibetan language-speaking ethnic groups who live mainly in Myanmar and Thailand

Kurdish: also called Kurds; an Iranian ethnic group that inhabits the mountainous region of Western Asia typically referred to as Kurdistan

Lasagna: originated in Italy in the 14th century and now popular in the US and around the world; type of layered pasta dish made with flat pasta, tomato sauce, and cheese

Latinos: a term to refer to people with cultural ties to Latin America

Latinos Unidos: a group of students working to raise awareness about Latino culture and the social issues affecting their community

Latinx: a gender-neutral term used at times instead of Latino or Latina

Layover: a period of time before the next stage of a journey, most commonly used when referring to waiting for a plane

LGBT: an acronym for individuals identifying as lesbian, gay, bisexual, transgender, or other sexual and gender identities who are unified through a common culture and social movements

Liberal Arts Transfer Program: a college-level program that assists students pursuing academic studies in the humanities, natural sciences, mathematics, or other social sciences

Longfellow High School: a school located in Milwaukee, Wisconsin

Machiques: fourth largest city in Zulia, Venezuela, located in the northwest area of the country near the border of Columbia

Mae Kaew Ka: a refugee camp located in northern Thailand

Mae La Oon: a refugee camp located in Sob Moei District, Mae Hong Son Province of Thailand with a population of approximately 9,000

Mae Sot: a district in western Thailand and trade hub substantiated by Burmese migrants and refugees

Managua: the capital city of Nicaragua located on the southwestern shore of Lake Managua with a population of approximately 1,000,000

Manali: a resort town of Himachal Pradesh state in India with a population of approximately 8,000

Manchester United: a professional football (soccer) club founded in 1878 and renamed in 1902 that plays in England's top-tier football league, the Premier League

Manga: a comic or graphic novel genre created in Japan

Maracaibo: located on the western shore of Venezuela, the city is the second largest city in the country with a population of approximately 1,500,000

María Luisa McDougall: an elementary school located in Guanica, Puerto Rico

Marines: a branch of the United States Armed Forces founded in November 1775; one of the four armed service branches under the US Department of Defense

Marquette University: a private research university in Milwaukee, Wisconsin, founded by the Society of Jesus in 1881 serving 11,600 undergraduate and graduate students

Mass: officially the Most Holy Sacrifice of the Mass; refers to the religious service in the Catholic Church where participants worship and partake in communion

Maungdaw: a town in Myanmar in the western part of the country, with a population of approximately 400,000

Mechanical engineering: a discipline that applies principles of engineering, physics, and material science to design, analyze, manufacture, and maintain mechanical systems

Militia: an organized military force formed from the civilian population that rebels or opposes a regular army

Milwaukee Area Technical College (MATC): a public two-year vocational-technical college located in Milwaukee, Wisconsin

Mindfulness Club: an organized group of students who learn and share techniques focused on being fully present to aid in strengthening one's well being; often includes meditation and other exercises that reduce stress and distractions

Mofongo: a Puerto Rican dish primarily consisting of fried plantains, mashed into a ball with other ingredients such as garlic, olive oil and pork rinds

Mole Poblano: a traditional dish in Mexican cuisine that consists of chili peppers and chococal as well as other native Mexican ingredients included tortillas, cilantro, and tomatillos

Monopoly: a popular American board game that focuses on using money to buy property while trying not to go bankrupt; first published by the Parker Brothers in 1935 and now currently published by Hasbro

Moombahton: a fusion of house music and reggaetón created by American DJ and producer Dave Nada in 2009

Naruto: a manga franchise made by Masashi Kishimoto in 1997 based around a young ninja named Naruto

Nicaraguan revolution: a significant period in Nicaragua's history. A revolution led by the Sandinista National Liberation Front (FSLN) against the opposing Somoza dictatorship in the 1960s and 1970s

Nikkah: a traditional Islamic marriage, legally recognized as a union between a man and a woman

Omoa: a town in the Department of Cortes on the Northwest Caribbean coast of Honduras with a population of approximately 47,000

Pasteles: a Puerto Rican dish that consists of a meat stew, packed into a special dough (called "masa") and wrapped in a banana leaf

Pathways Programs: programs sponsored by the US State Department designed to help international students at all levels improve English language fluency and writing to largely compete for jobs in the federal workforce

Pennsylvania: a state in the US located in the northeastern part of the country with population of approximately 12,000,000

PEOPLE Program: The acronym for "Pre-College Enrichment Opportunity Program for Learning Excellence;" the program is designed to increase college enrollment and graduation rates for students of color with lower-economic backgrounds and/or first-generation college attendees

Political asylum: individuals who are considered political refugees after leaving their native country are granted protection by a receiving nation

Power Rangers: an American television series and entertainment franchise released in 1993 by Saban Entertainment and is now owned by Hasbro

Progressive house: a subgenre of house music that emerged in the early 1990s in the United Kingdom

Puebla, Mexico: a city in Mexico located in central Mexico with a population of approximately 1,000,000

Quetta: the capital of Balochistan, Pakistan with a population approximately 1,000,000

Quinceañera: a celebration of a girl's fifteenth birthday in Hispanic cultures

Quran (Koran): the sacred and primary primary religious text of Islam; revealed to the Prophet Muhammad by the the archangel Gabriel over twenty-three years from 609 to 632 CE; considered a divine revelation by God

Rakhine State: a state in Myanmar on the western coast, with a population of approximately 3,000,000

Refugee camp: a temporary settlement to accommodate individuals facing displacement due to war, economic, or environmental reasons; typically overseen by a government, the United Nations, international relief organizations, or NGOs

Registered Nurse (RN): a person who holds a nursing diploma from an accredited nursing program and who has passed a national exam to obtain a license

Rohingya: a Indo-Aryan Ethnic group that resides in Rakhine State of Myanmar, many of whom are refugees fleeing their home but are denied citizenship in countries like Bangladesh, because of the 1982 Myanmar nationality law that does not recognize them as one of the eight indigenous races

Ronaldo: a reference to Cristiano Ronaldo, a Portuguese football (soccer) player and sports celebrity affiliated with the Juventus Football Club

Santa Claus: a Western Christian legendary and mythical character who wears a red suit, has a white beard, and resides in the North Pole; also known as Kris Kringle, Father Christmas, and Saint Nicolas, he is celebrated in stories where he delivers toys children on Christmas Eve

Swahili: a Bantu language and lingua franca (common language understood and used) of many countries in the African Great Lake regions and parts of eastern and south-eastern African countries including Kenya, Uganda, and Rwanda

Target: the eighth-largest retail chain-store company in the United States, founded in 1902; sells groceries and merchandise throughout the US in approximately 1,850 stores

TCV: a nonprofit organization called the Tibetan Children's Villages that helps orphans and refugees with education, located in northern India and run by the Central Tibetan Administration

Tegucigalpa: often referred to as Téguz; the capital and largest city of Honduras with a population of approximately 1,000,000

Tibet: a historical region of the Tibetan Plateau located on the continent of Asia; the highest region on earth, its highest elevation being Mount Everest

Tigris River: a 1,150 mile-long river flowing south from Turkey through Iraq and into the Persian Gulf; the eastern border of the region of Mesopotamia

Traditional food (from Venezuela): Examples include—arepa, which is composed of cooked flour or ground corn/maize that resembles flat bread or cake and contains taco-style fillings like tomato, meat, or vegetables; cachapa, which is a lumpier and thicker form of pancake composed of corn kernel

Trap music: a style of hip hop music that was developed in the late 1990s in southern United States

Twi: a dialect of the Akan language that is recognized as one of the official languages of the country of Ghana

U-Haul: an American moving, storage, and rental equipment company founded in Arizona in 1945; primarily recognized as a rental truck company for US consumers

UNO: a card game

US Embassy: the official headquarters for US Government representatives who are working abroad

Verona: a city in the state of Wisconsin with a population of approximately 10,000

Visa Provision: a temporary visa provided by the state to allow an individual temporary access into the United States

Wii U: a gaming console developed by Nintendo that can handle HD graphics, released in 2012 to be the more-advanced successor of the Nintendo Wii

Woodman's: also called Woodman's Markets; an American supermarket chain founded in 1919 and based in Wisconsin

Yoga: an ancient physical, mental, and spiritual practice and discipline originating in India in circa 3,000; strongly affiliated with Hinduism as well as Buddhism, and Jainism; modern yoga is a popular fitness and wellness practice throughout the world

About Green Card Voices

Founded in 2013, Green Card Voices is a Minneapolis-based, nationally growing social enterprise that works to record and share first person narratives of America's immigrants to facilitate a better understanding between immigrants and their communities. Our dynamic, multimedia platform, book collections, and traveling exhibits are designed to empower educational institutions, community groups, and individuals to acquire first-person perspectives about immigrants' lives, increasing appreciation of immigrant experiences in America.

Green Card Voices was born from the idea that the broad narrative of current immigrants should be communicated in a way that is true to each immigrant's story. We seek to be a new lens for those in the immigration dialogue and to build bridges between newcomers and their receiving communities across the country. We do this by sharing the firsthand immigration stories of foreign-born Americans, and by helping others to see each "wave of immigrants" as individuals with valuable stories of family, hard work, and cultural diversity.

To date, the Green Card Voices team has recorded the life stories of over four hundred immigrants coming from more than one hundred and twenty different countries. All immigrants who decide to share their story with GCV are asked six open-ended questions. The recorded narratives are edited down to five-minute videos, available on www.greencardvoices.org, and social media.

Immigration Stories from Madison and Milwaukee High Schools is the fifth book to be published in the *Green Card Youth Voices series*. It followed books featuring students from an Atlanta, Minneapolis, Fargo, and St. Paul High Schools. Green Card Voices has also published *Green Card Entrepreneur Voices: How-To Business Stories from Minnesota Immigrants,* and *Green Card STEM Voices: Stories from Minnesota Immigrants Working in Science, Technology, Engineering, and Math.*

Contact information:
Green Card Voices
Minneapolis, MN
www.greencardvoices.org
612.889.7635

facebook.com/greencardvoices
twitter.com/greencardvoices
instagram.com/greencardvoices
linkedin.com/company/green-card-voices

Immigrant Youth Traveling Exhibits

Twenty students' stories from each city in the *Green Card Youth* series (Madison/ Milwaukee, Atlanta, Minneapolis, Fargo, and St. Paul) are featured in traveling exhibits, available to schools, universities, libraries, and other venues where communities gather. Each exhibit features twenty stories from a particular city, each with a portrait, a 200-word biography, and a quote from each immigrant. A QR code is displayed next to each portrait and can be scanned with a mobile device to watch the digital stories. The following programming can be provided with the exhibit: panel discussions, presentations, and community-building events.

Green Card Voices also coordinates a National Exhibit featuring all six cities. This exhibit is available for rental across the country.

Green Card Voices currently has seven exhibits based on different communities across the Midwest and South. To rent an exhibit, please contact us at 612.889.7635 or info@greencardvoices.org.

Green Card Youth Voices: Book Readings

Meeting the student authors in person creates a dynamic space in which to engage with these topics firsthand. Book readings are a wonderful opportunity to hear the students share their stories and answer questions about their lived experiences.

To schedule a book reading in your area, please contact us at 612.889.7635 or info@greencardvoices.org.

Order Through Our Distributor

Our books and Story Stitch are distributed in the US & Canada by Consortium Book Sales & Distribution, an Ingram Company.

For orders and customer care in the U.S., contact:

Phone: 866.400.5351
PCI Secure Fax (orders only): 731.424.0988
Email (orders only): ips@ingramcontent.com
Online: ipage.ingramcontent.com
Electronic orders: IPS SAN 6318630

Mail: Ingram Publisher Services
Attn: Customer Care
1 Ingram Blvd., Box 512, La Vergne, TN 37086
Hours: Monday–Friday
        8:00 am to 5:00 pm CST

For orders and customer service in Canada, contact:

Phone: 800.663.5714
Email: orders@raincoastbooks.com

Green Card Voices Store

Immigration Stories from a
Minneapolis High School
ISBN: 978-1-949523-00-3

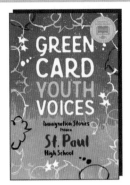

Immigration Stories from a
St. Paul High School
ISBN: 978-1-949523-04-1

Immigration Stories from
a Fargo High School
ISBN: 978-1-949523-02-7

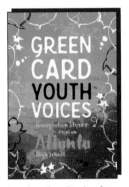

Immigration Stories from
an Atlanta High School
ISBN: 978-1-949523-05-8

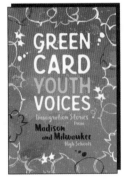

Immigration Stories from Madison
& Milwaukee High Schools
ISBN: 978-1-949523-12-6

Voices of Immigrant
Storytellers Teaching Guide
for Middle & High Schools
ISBN: 978-0-692572-81-8

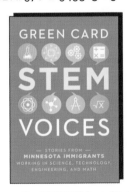

Green Card STEM Voices: Stories
from Minnesota Immigrants
Working in Science, Technology,
Engineering, and Math
ISBN: 978-1-949523-14-0

Green Card Entrepreneur
Voices: How-To Business
Stories from Minnesota
Immigrants
ISBN: 978-1-949523-07-2

Story Stitch: Telling Stories,
Opening Minds, Becoming
Neighbors
ISBN: 978-1-949523-11-9

Purchase at our online store: *www.greencardvoices.org/store*